SAVORY BAKING

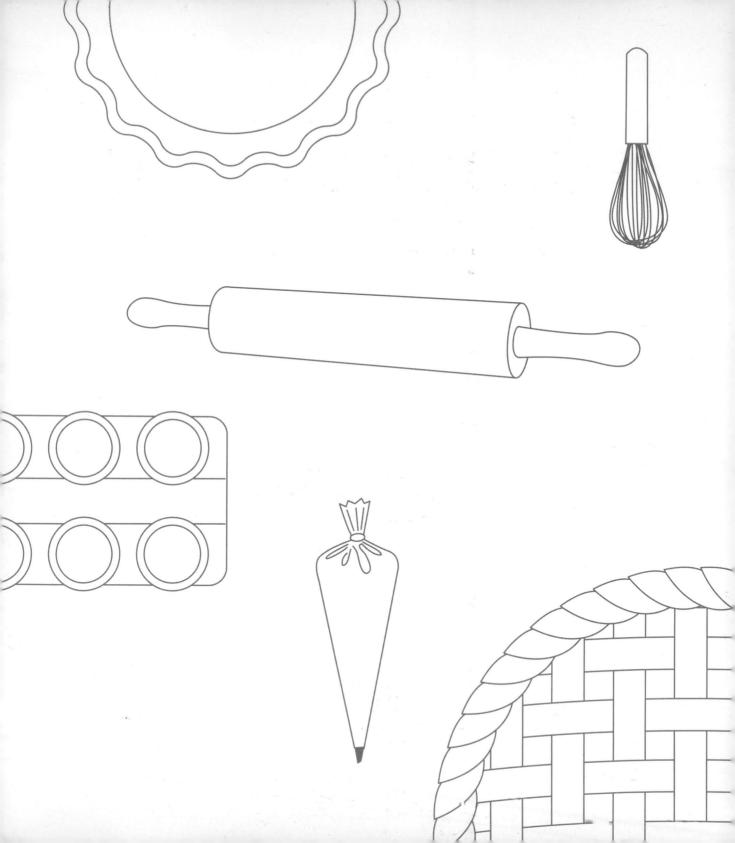

SAVORY BAKING

WARM AND INSPIRING RECIPES FOR CRISP, CRUMBLY, FLAKY PASTRIES

By Mary Cech ◆ Photographs by Noel Barnhurst

CHRONICLE BOOKS
SAN FRANCISCO

Library of Congress Cataloging-in-Publication Data available.

ISBN 978-0-8118-5906-6

Manufactured in China.

Prop styling by
GEORGE DOLESE

Food styling by
GEORGE DOLESE
ELISABET DER NEDERLANDEN

Design by
ELOISE LEIGH

Typesetting by
ELOISE LEIGH

The photographer wishes to thank his assistants:
ANGELINA CANTADA
RENEE DODGE
LUKE GOODMAN

10 9 8 7 6 5 4 3 2 1

Chronicle Books LLC
680 Second Street
San Francisco, California 94107

www.chroniclebooks.com

Bundt cake pans is a registered trademark of Northland Aluminum Products, Inc.
King Arthur Flour is a registered trademark of the King Arthur Flour Company, Inc.
Microplane grater is a registered trademark of Grace Manufacturing, Inc.
Play-Doh is a registered trademark of Hasbro, Inc.
Pomi canned tomatoes is a registered trademark of Boschi Food & Beverages S.P.A.
Tetra Pak is a registered trademark of Tetra Laval Holdings & Finance S.A

◄ DEDICATION ►

To the man who will try "at least one bite" of everything I bake and cook,
my husband, Elliott.

◄ ACKNOWLEDGMENTS ►

I am truly grateful for my good friends, loving family, and trusting colleagues who believe in me and have contributed to the reality and success of this book. Without their assistance, support, and instructional knowledge, *Savory Baking* would still only be a dream.

I thank my agent, Doe Coover, once again, for a successful collaboration with Chronicle Books. I am grateful to Bill LeBlond and Amy Treadwell for their continued belief and editorial support. For additional editorial suggestions, I thank Barbara Schwalm for how easy she made editing appear to me. Her positive attitude and willingness to give me helpful writing suggestions comforted me during my writing process.

To the many recipe testers whose palates, knowledge, and comments brought so many valuable cooking and baking suggestions, variations, and thought provoking notes to every recipe they tested: I gratefully thank you; it was fun working together! I especially thank Shellie Kark, former chef de cuisine of Cook Street School of Fine Cooking in Denver, Colorado. She brought an ease and enthusiasm to all the recipes she tested. She provided me with an unspoken feeling of comfort as I tiptoed into the less-comfortable territory of savory cooking. Thanks to Sheryl, Peggy, and Marguerite who, with their discerning palates, provided me with texture and flavor suggestions along with sea-level alterations.

I thank all the tasters whom I inundated with samples for months: Barbara, Nancy, Patty, Stephanie, Carol, Debbie, Letty, Paul, and Crystal.

Thank you to Deer Valley Resort and the Sky Lodge resort for understanding the time commitments of a cookbook project; you graciously provided me with flexible schedules, willing testers and tasters, and overall support.

A heartfelt thank-you to everyone for your inspiring enthusiasm; your assistance is reflected within the pages of this book.

CONTENTS

RUSTIC ◆ 83
COBBLERS, CRUMBLES, BETTIES, BREAD PUDDINGS, SHORTCAKES, DUMPLINGS, AND CHEESECAKES

THE SIDE SHOW ◆ 141
SAUCES, SPREADS, CHUTNEYS, AND SALADS

INTRODUCTION

WHILE TEACHING culinary classes across the country, I have observed an overwhelming number of students who love to bake. My baking classes have drawn a large but specific group of eager individuals, mostly sweets-lovers. Other students equally as enthusiastic about cooking seemed to shy away from baking. Why was this? My inquiries told me either the intimidation of baking was overwhelming or not everyone had a sweet tooth. These thoughts subconsciously resonated in me for several years.

I STARTED NOTICING a subtle and natural transition in my class recipes as sugar and spice began taking a back burner to fresh herbs and other savory ingredients. Pastries took on a new life as I layered, wrapped, and covered them with robust woodsy mushrooms, hearty smoked meats, creamy cheeses, and spring-fresh vegetables and served them with spoonfuls of interesting sauces and condiments.

My sweet-tooth pastry world was beginning to transform and intertwine with one of savory offerings for anytime fare. It seemed natural to nibble on cheese pastry sticks with ice-cold champagne at the beginning of a class. Puffy soufflés dotted with mushrooms and scented with garlic became a light lunchtime favorite. Students filled classes to try my caramelized onion pizza covered with paper-thin new potato slices and Gruyère.

ALTHOUGH SWEET PASTRY baking will always be a big part of my culinary pleasures, I enjoy the creativity and sense of adventure when incorporating savory ingredients into baking and sharing warm-from-the-oven goodies with my students, friends, and family any time, not just for dessert! *Savory Baking* was created with the intention of bringing baking and cooking together in mouth-watering recipes. It offers all cooks and bakers an opportunity to experience the synergy between the world of cooking and the world of baking. My book fills a niche and satisfies the appetites of every pastry maker and every adventurous home cook who strives to bake successfully.

READERS WILL DISCOVER new recipe options, as well as ideas that expand on their own favorite dishes. Pastry recipes usually reserved for dessert and breakfast now take center stage as savory appetizers, entrées, snacks, and side dishes. Understanding hectic schedules, I have included tips for preparing and storing recipe components ahead of time, which will make evenings of cooking a breeze.

THE TOOLS FOR SUCCESS section includes time-saving ideas and lists prepared foods, ingredients, equipment, and cooking and baking techniques, all helpful in creating a pleasant and successful cooking

experience. A glossary explains the book's baking and cooking terms.

THERE IS A RECIPE for everyone within my book, from simple Crispy Potato Haystacks (page 126) to dramatic and creative dishes, such as Caesar Tartlets with Sweet Garlic–Butter Crusts (page 58). Explore my book and you will find six chapters containing 72 inviting recipes to engage everyone from the less-experienced cook or novice baker to the more-advanced home cook. I invite you to have fun and make some of these recipes your new favorites.

TOOLS FOR SUCCESS

INGREDIENTS—FRESH AND PREPARED

I recommend making all of my recipes from scratch with the finest fresh and seasonal ingredients. However, good-quality prepared foods come in all forms and are convenient for today's busy lifestyles. Jarred, canned, frozen, and boxed products line the shelves of the most basic supermarkets and gourmet markets. These prepared foods can help even the busiest cook save time in the kitchen and can encourage home cooking and baking to flourish.

BUTTER

Use the best-quality butter that fits easily into your budget. Grades AA and A are most commonly found at the retail level. All recipes in this book call for unsalted butter. "Sweet" butter usually means salted butter. Be careful not to confuse the two. If you are not sure, read the label for clarification.

CHEESE

Most cheeses in this book are easy to find at the supermarket. Cheeses used for cooking lend themselves well to savory baking and blend nicely with other ingredients. Blue cheese, cream cheese, goat, Jack, mozzarella, Parmesan, ricotta, and Swiss cheeses are among some of the most popular used for baking. They add flavor to a batter or dough, especially when sugar has been removed from a recipe for a savory application. Shred or grate your own (see page 18 for grating and shredding techniques) or buy it preshredded.

CHINESE FIVE-SPICE POWDER

Widely available in supermarkets, in Asian markets, and online, this powder is a blend of spices that includes cloves, fennel, ginger, ground cinnamon, licorice root, star anise, and white pepper.

CHUTNEY

This spicy condiment comes in all textures, degrees of spiciness, and flavor combinations. Chutney makes an interesting bread spread and is delicious served with cheese. It is a great accompaniment to many of the dishes in this book. Jarred chutney is available in most supermarkets, specialty markets, and Indian food markets.

CRÈME FRAÎCHE

Crème fraîche is thickened cream with a slightly tangy, nutty flavor and a velvety-rich texture. It can be found in many markets, but it can be costly. You can easily make your own (page 149) or substitute equal amounts of sour cream in a recipe that calls for crème fraîche.

CURRY POWDER

This dry spice typically contains a mixture of cloves, coriander, cumin, ground red pepper, and turmeric. Commercial curry powder comes in two main styles—standard and Madras, which is hotter. Commercial curry powders vary significantly, however, so try them to see which you prefer.

EGGS

Large grade A eggs are used in all of my recipes that call for eggs. Leftover egg yolks can be covered with a little cold water, tightly wrapped, and refrigerated for up to 3 days. They freeze well when $1/8$ teaspoon of salt or $1\frac{1}{2}$ teaspoons of sugar per $1/4$ cup of egg yolks is stirred into them before freezing. If the yolks are frozen without the salt or sugar, they will become lumpy and unusable. An easy way to freeze egg whites is to place one in each section of an ice cube tray. Freeze, then pop them out and thaw and use them as you need.

FENNEL

Sweet fennel is an herb, but it is used as a vegetable. It has a large, bulblike base, hollow stalks, and threadlike leaves. Its sweet and delicate flavor is similar to that of licorice. When cooked, its flavor becomes lighter and more delicate. Sweet fennel is available fall through spring. Select unblemished, clean, crisp bulbs with no sign of browning. Any attached greenery should be a fresh bright green color. The whole plant can be used, either cooked or raw, in any recipe calling for celery. Store fennel in a plastic bag, wrapped tightly, and refrigerate for up to five days.

FLOUR

I have chosen King Arthur unbleached all-purpose flour for all recipes that call for all-purpose flour. There is no need to sift the flour unless a recipe specifically calls for sifting. King Arthur flour is easily found in supermarkets.

ITALIAN TOMATOES

Canned Italian tomatoes are readily available. They come whole, chopped, diced, and puréed. I prefer the rich, full flavor of Pomi brand tomatoes for many of my recipes. You can find them packed in Tetra Pak boxes.

JAPANESE BREAD CRUMBS

Also called panko bread crumbs, these are sometimes found in the fresh fish department, and at other times, with the baking goods. Look for Japanese bread crumbs in boxes, in 1-pound canisters, or in bulk.

PESTO

Although Italian pesto is usually made with fresh basil leaves and pine nuts, it can be made with an assortment of ingredients that will create a paste with unique flavors. Classic pesto, sun-dried tomato pesto, and walnut pesto are a few of the variations available at supermarkets, specialty markets, and online.

PHYLLO PASTRY DOUGH

Often labeled "filo" dough, phyllo dough can be found in the freezer department of supermarkets or in many Middle Eastern markets. Phyllo dough purchased in supermarkets comes in 1-pound boxes. Sometimes a 1-pound box will contain one roll, other times a 1-pound box will contain two 8-ounce individually wrapped rolls. All of my recipes call for phyllo dough sheets from 1-pound boxes with two 8-ounce packages. The sheets are 13 by 9 inches in size. If your supermarket only carries 1-pound rolls, cut the dough sheets to the size specified in each recipe. Phyllo can be stored in the refrigerator for up to 1 month if it is wrapped airtight. Once the airtight packaging has been opened, use it within a few days. This delicately thin dough can easily dry out and become excessively crumbly, making it difficult to work with.

POTATOES

With all the different varieties of potatoes available, how do you decide which to use in a recipe? Choose potatoes based on how you are going to use them. High-starch varieties, such as russet and Idaho potatoes, yield a light and fluffy texture that is great for baking, frying, and mashing. Low-starch potatoes, such as fingerling, new potatoes (all small, waxy potatoes), red skinned, and Yukon, are known for their creamy, buttery texture. They hold their shape after cooking, which makes them an excellent choice for boiling, roasting, and scalloping and for use in potato salads.

PREPARED PIE PASTRY AND PIE SHELLS

Pie dough pastry is an unsweetened dough that is great for both sweet and savory applications. It can be found already rolled into 8- or 9-inch aluminum pie pans at most supermarkets and specialty markets. A variety of brand-name prerolled shells ready for baking can be located in the freezer department. You will also find prerolled packaged pastry, for lining your own pie pans, in the refrigerator case.

PREPARED PUFF PASTRY DOUGH

Sheets of puff pastry dough generally come in 1-pound boxes and can be found in your grocer's freezer department. Look for all-butter puff pastry, which will have a superior flavor after it has been baked.

ROASTED PEPPERS

Roasted red and yellow bell peppers come packed in water or oil. They are found in most markets.

SUN-DRIED TOMATOES

Usually dried in the sun or by other methods, these deep-flavored tomatoes are sweet and dark red. They are packed in oil or dry-packed in cellophane. Recipes in this book call for oil-packed sun-dried tomatoes, which are found in most markets.

SWEETENERS

A few recipes in this book call for small amounts of sugar, corn syrup, or honey. Rather than make a baked item sweet, sweeteners are intended to enhance and bring out the flavor of other ingredients in a baked product. Sugar is used sparingly and in balance with a recipe, much like salt.

TAPENADE

A flavorful, thick olive paste, tapenade is used as a condiment and is easily found in most supermarkets, in specialty markets, and online.

A WORD ABOUT WATER

I usually do not calculate an exact amount of water in puff pastry or pie pastry dough recipes. Depending on climate, altitude, and the freshness of the flour, the dough will absorb a slightly different amount of water each time it is made. Look for freshly mixed dough to be moist, but not wet. If it is dry and crumbly, a bit more water should be added in the mixing process. If the dough is sticky, too much water has already been added. If you choose not to start over, know that the dough may be a bit hard to work with and slightly tough when baked.

EQUIPMENT

Not all kitchen gadgets and equipment need to be the most expensive, but investing in sturdy, high-quality tools will help to simplify cooking tasks and save time. Stand mixers, food processors, kitchen knives, and heavy-gauge pots, pans, and baking sheets will last for years, if handled with care. They can help you produce properly mixed batters, consistently chopped nuts, and evenly baked biscuits and cookies.

BAKING PANS

Try to use the size pan specified in each recipe, regardless of its material. A heavier pan is preferred, as it retains the heat better. In general, shiny and pale materials reflect heat and will produce tender, delicately crusted, lighter-colored pastries. Dark nonstick or glass bakeware will produce a thicker, crisper, and darker crust, best for baking the bottom crust of a pie.

BAKING SHEETS

Sometimes referred to as jellyroll pans, cookie sheets, and sheet pans, baking sheets come in a variety of sizes and thicknesses. Make sure your sheets are medium- to heavy-gauge aluminum and at least $1/16$ inch thick to ensure they don't buckle in a hot oven.

CRÊPE PAN

This is a classic shallow round pan usually made of carbon steel or anodized aluminum, with a long handle to allow cooks to tilt the pan to ensure the batter coats the bottom as thinly as possible. A small, heavyweight, nonstick skillet about 7 or 8 inches in diameter is a good alternative to a crêpe pan.

ELECTRIC MIXERS AND THEIR ATTACHMENTS

A stand mixer is an invaluable kitchen tool that makes easy work of creaming butter and cream cheese with the paddle attachment or whipping air into egg whites with the whisk attachment. In many cases, when recipes in this book call for an electric mixer, or a stand mixer, a food processor may be used instead. If you don't have a stand mixer, a handheld electric mixer can be useful for whipping air into ingredients, such as egg whites and heavy cream, whereas a food processor won't do the job correctly.

FOOD PROCESSOR

For some things, like finely grinding nuts or quickly and efficiently making pastry dough, a food processor is indispensable. Choose a brand with a sturdy and powerful motor and a large bowl.

GRATERS AND RASPS

Handheld graters and zesters make easy work for a number of cooking tasks, from finely zesting citrus rind to grating piles of hard and medium-hard cheeses. When recipes in this book call for "finely grated" or "zested" ingredients, I used a handheld grater called a Microplane.

MADELEINE MOLDS

These special rectangular molds have 12 standard-size or 24 mini indentations that resemble elongated scallop shells. Choose heavy-duty trays made of tinned steel or aluminum.

METAL SPREADING UTENSILS

These types of tools may be flat or bent at the mid-point. The flat version is called a palette knife and is good for spreading a variety of batters and creams. The bent type is called an offset palette knife and is excellent for delicate spreading jobs or for adding leverage when lifting fragile items like tarts and cake slices.

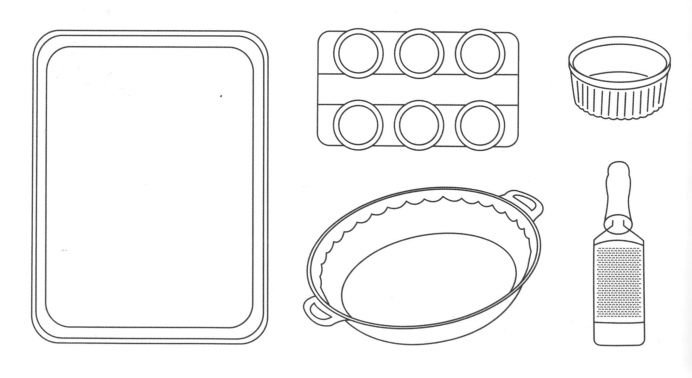

PASTRY BAGS

I prefer the disposable plastic type commonly available in cookware stores. These bags avoid potential contamination with previously used ingredients. The bags come in a variety of sizes and can be cut to fit the particular pastry tip needed for the job. If you do not have a pastry bag, spoon a small amount of dough onto one of two spoons. With the other spoon, push the dough off onto the baking sheet.

PIE PANS

I prefer metal dark pans, uncoated or nonstick, as they absorb heat, which helps to bake a bottom crust completely.

PIE WEIGHTS

When a prebaked pie shell is called for in a recipe, use pie weights to hold the pastry in place as it is baking, preventing it from rising and blistering (see Blind Baking, page 23). You can buy ceramic or metal pie weights, but dried beans, rice, or peas work just as well, and they can be reused after they have cooled. Keep them in a well-labeled airtight jar so they are not mistaken for your soup! Store beans, rice, or peas that have been used as pie weights for up to 3 months, then throw them out because they will become rancid.

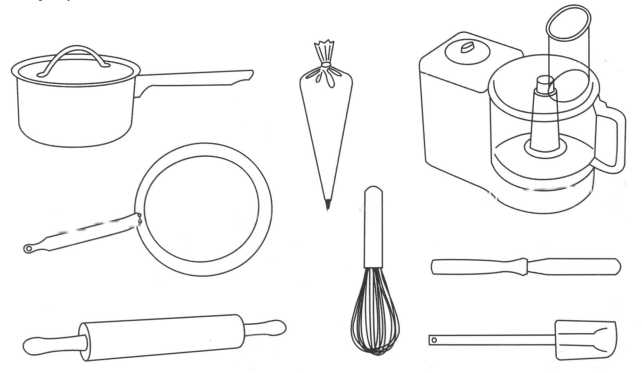

POPOVER PANS

These pans, usually available in gourmet cookware shops, are made of heavy-duty black steel and are sometimes called Yorkshire pudding pans. They have six 4-inch-deep oval cups suspended from a wire frame. Other pans can be used to make popovers, but the finished popover won't have such a dramatically tall and stunning look. Good popover pan alternatives are muffin cups, 3-by-2-inch heavy-gauge aluminum baba molds, or individual heat-proof porcelain soufflé dishes that are 3$\frac{1}{3}$ by 2 inches in size.

RAMEKINS AND OTHER BAKING MOLDS

Ramekins and other ceramic baking dishes come in a wide assortment of shapes and sizes. They are useful for baking sweet and savory custards, soufflés, and casseroles in large family-style or individual portions. Ramekins can be plain white or a wide range of colors and shapes that allow them to double as decorative serving dishes. To measure the capacity of your ramekins, fill one with water and pour it into a measuring cup. An 8-ounce ramekin will hold 1 cup of water; a 6-ounce ramekin will hold ¾ cup of water.

RICER

Also called a potato ricer, this kitchen utensil resembles a large garlic press. Cooked foods, usually vegetables, are placed in the container and a lever-operated plunger is pushed down on the food, forcing it out tiny holes in the bottom of the container. Ricers are generally made of chromed steel or cast aluminum and are found in specialty cookware shops.

ROLLING PINS

Many rolling pin variations are available. My preference is for a traditional wooden rolling pin with handles and ball bearings to roll dough. The dough rolls evenly with less pressure on the palms of my hands.

RUBBER SPATULAS

The rubber spatulas called for in this book have durable, long plastic handles and flexible, flat rubber blades. They are good for scraping bowls and folding and stirring ingredients together. I prefer a heat-resistant variety of spatula.

SAUCEPANS

Anodized aluminum is popular for domestic cookware. The aluminum for this material has been electrochemically sealed, making it nonreactive and extremely hard. These pans are excellent heat conductors. The best stainless-steel pots are either fortified with copper bottoms or made of a layer of aluminum sandwiched between two layers of stainless steel. Unfortified stainless steel heats unevenly and can scorch sauces.

SILICONE BAKING MATS AND PARCHMENT PAPER

Silicone baking mats are widely available for home use and come in two sizes. They are easily cleaned, can be used repeatedly, and are excellent for lining baking sheets. These stick-resistant mats are especially useful for baking very thin cookies and wafers, which peel off the mats much more easily than they would from other types of nonstick paper. Parchment paper is ready to use and needs no preparation. It is usually purchased in rolls or sheets for lining baking pans and comes in a variety of sizes that conveniently fit the bottom of many round cake pans.

SKILLETS

One large skillet is essential for most cooks. Skillets are good for sautéing and caramelizing fruits, meats, and vegetables, giving them plenty of room to contact the wide surface. I prefer a 12- to 14-inch skillet that does not have a nonstick finish, as the coating tends to prevent proper caramelization of food. I also like a nonstick 7-inch skillet, which is excellent for smaller or delicate jobs and can double as a crêpe pan.

TART AND TARTLET PANS

Many French and European tarts are made in these classic pans. Most tart pans are made of tinned steel, with ribbed or fluted rims. They should feel heavy and strong. One round 9-inch pan is essential and is the standard size for most large tarts. Recipes using individual tart pans usually call for 4-inch pans. Make sure to purchase pans with removable bottoms for easy removal of your tarts. They are commonly used and widely available.

WHISKS

There are two main types of whisks available. The sauce whisk is long and narrow with thick, stiff wires and a tapered bottom. The balloon whisk is made of finer, more flexible wires. Having one of each in your kitchen is essential.

A NOTE ABOUT TIME
AND TEMPERATURE

The baking and cooking times as well as the cooking temperatures suggested in the recipes will vary slightly in every kitchen. Consider these recommended cooking and baking times in the recipes as "average doneness guidelines" that will help you know what to look for. Following are some temperature and doneness guidelines to help you cook and bake successfully.

Check for doneness at least 5 minutes before the suggested time.

If a recipe suggests that you "bake until golden brown and the top springs back gently when pressed in the center with your finger," but you find those doneness criteria are met in 35 minutes rather than the recipe's suggested 40 to 45 minutes, remove the baked item from the oven.

If the recommended baking temperature is 400°F but the item is quickly browning and beginning to burn within the first 10 minutes, turn the temperature down 25 degrees.

If a baked item is not done in the suggested 45 minutes, continue checking every 5 minutes until it reaches the indicated degree of doneness. This is the best way to ensure reliable results.

If a recipe suggests to "sauté until translucent on high heat" and burning occurs rapidly, turn the flame down to a lower heat.

MASTERING BAKING AND COOKING TECHNIQUES FOR SUCCESS

Read the recipe at least once before you begin to bake or cook to avoid any surprises. Be sure to preheat the oven to the correct temperature when and as indicated in the recipe. Have all the right equipment and ingredients available. Understand all the techniques before you start. Carefully measure all of the ingredients first and double-check that you have premeasured every item in the ingredients list. Follow the recipe as written and in the order given. All of these tips and the ones that follow will help you enjoy a pleasant and successful baking and cooking experience. Most of all, have fun!

BLIND BAKING

This is a method used for prebaking a crust, either partially or completely, before filling. I prefer to bake a pie crust shell completely golden brown before gently baking a delicate custard inside, such as for quiche. To blind bake, line the raw pastry shell with aluminum foil or parchment paper about 2 inches larger than the rim of the pan. Fill the liner to the top with pie weights (see page 19). In an oven preheated to 400°F, bake the pie shell on the bottom rack for 30 minutes. Carefully lift a corner of the foil to check the bottom for doneness. When the bottom is beginning to brown, remove the shell from the oven, as well as the liner and weights. At this point, the crust is partially blind baked. To completely blind bake, return the shell to the oven and bake until

golden brown, an additional 5 to 10 minutes. If any puffing of the pastry shell occurs during the last 5 to 10 minutes gently tap the bubbles down with a kitchen or paper towel.

CRÊPE BAKING

Make sure your batter is smooth and has the consistency of heavy cream. A thin batter is desirable because it will spread over the pan easily. I like a quick spray of cooking oil on the pan between making each crêpe, but melted butter lightly brushed in the pan works just as well. Heat your pan over medium-high heat until hot but not smoking. Remove the pan from the heat, immediately ladle 3 to 4 tablespoons (about ¼ cup) of batter into one corner of the pan, and then tilt and rotate the pan quickly in all directions to coat the entire surface evenly with the batter. (If the batter does not spread quickly, it's too thick and needs to be thinned with a little milk or water.) If you have too much batter, simply pour the excess back into the bowl after swirling. In about 1 minute, the edges of the crêpe will be lightly browned and will lift up slightly from the pan. The top will look almost dry and set. Slide a long spatula around the rim of the pan and turn the crêpe carefully. Cook briefly on the other side, 15 to 30 seconds. The resulting crêpe should remain soft and barely browned. Invert the pan and release the crêpe onto a clean dish towel or plate. The process goes quickly once you get the hang of it. Continue to make the crêpes, stacking them on top of each other. Crêpes can be wrapped tightly and refrigerated for 3 days, or frozen for up to 1 month.

DEEP FRYING

The best type of pot for the fried dough recipes in this book is a heavy one with sides that are at least 3 inches high. The fat for frying should be at least 2 inches deep. The temperature should be about 375°F and can be measured with a candy thermometer clipped to the side of the pot with the bulb ½ inch from the bottom of the pot. Leave the thermometer in the oil while cooking so you can constantly check the temperature. If the temperature of the oil is 10 degrees or more below what is recommended, the fried item will be heavy and greasy; too high, and the outside will overcook before the inside can catch up. After cooking each batch of dough, check to see if the temperature is accurate. If not, be patient; don't fry any additional dough until the temperature rises back up. Carefully place pieces of dough into the oil. Don't drop dough pieces in from above the surface, as you could splash hot oil over the stove and on yourself. Be careful not to overcrowd the pot as this lowers the oil temperature; leave space for each piece to float freely and expand as it cooks. Cook each piece of dough on both sides until golden brown, then carefully remove with a slotted spoon and place onto an absorbent paper towel–lined baking sheet. Put warm fried dough in a preheated oven (about 325°F) to keep warm while continuing to fry any remaining dough.

GRATED AND SHREDDED CHEESE

Typical measurement charts indicate that 4 ounces of shredded cheese measures 1 cup. However, grated cheese and shredded cheese measure different quantities, and I have chosen to finely grate cheese in many of my recipes using a rasp-type grater called a Microplane. Therefore, be sure to follow the recipes as directed for "finely grated" (hand grated with a rasp-type grater) or "shredded" (prepackaged and prepared).

RICING

This is a process for creating a light and fluffy texture (usually for potatoes) that makes it easy to combine with other ingredients, such as cream and butter for mashed potatoes. The best way to do this is to peel the potatoes, cut them into chunks, and cook them until tender. Let the potatoes cool enough to be handled and place them in the ricer cup. Press the lever down to squeeze the potatoes into a bowl. The resulting potatoes will look similar to garlic pressed from a garlic press.

ROASTING

When meat, poultry, or fish are roasted in the oven, a well-browned exterior and moist interior are produced. To roast vegetables, clean them, cut them, place them in an ovenproof baking dish, and cover, then cook until fork-tender. They can be roasted with a variety of herbs and spices. To roast bell peppers, place them on a foil-lined baking sheet and lightly coat them with olive oil. Broil them until the skin is blackened all over, turning frequently. Remove the blackened peppers from the oven and put them in a bowl. Cover the bowl tightly with the aluminum foil from the baking sheet. Let them steam for 5 minutes. When they are cool enough to be handled, peel off the charred skin and discard along with the seeds and stems. Roasted peppers can be covered and stored in the refrigerator for several days before use.

TOASTING NUTS

Something magical happens to nuts when they are toasted. Their taste and texture transform, and unique flavors make them richer and sweeter. In general, in a 325°F oven, nuts will take 8 to 12 minutes to toast depending on the type of nut. Some nuts, like macadamia and pine nuts, have a high oil content and tend to burn easily, so keep an eye on them when toasting. Toast nuts on a plain rimmed baking sheet in a single layer. Shake or turn them occasionally for even toasting. A few minutes in the oven masks natural nut tannins and any bitterness. Darker-toasted nuts have the richest flavor but take care not to burn them, which can turn the nuts bitter.

WATER BATH

A water bath is used to prevent custards, bread puddings, and cheesecakes from overbaking around the edges or cracking in the centers. To create a water bath, nest the baking mold inside a larger pan. Pour hot water into the outer pan; this insulates the food, creates moisture in the oven, and allows the food to gently bake.

ZESTING CITRUS

Use a rasp grater to gently zest only the outermost part of the citrus fruit. All of the oil and flavor are in the surface of the rind. The white pith underneath the surface is bitter.

CRUMBLE TOPPINGS

These toppings contain a balance of enough butter, sugar, and flour to make them dry and crumbly. They can be mixed with fingertips, in a food processor, or with a stand mixer. Sometimes rolled oats and spices are added and brown sugar is substituted for the white sugar.

PÂTE À CHOUX

This is a very versatile dough, puffy and hollow centered, that is neutral in flavor and used for both sweet and savory applications. It is twice cooked—first on the stovetop and then baked in the oven to create a crisp shell good for stuffing with assorted fillings. The dough is made of water or milk, butter, flour, and eggs. Sometimes a dash of sugar or salt will be added to a recipe as a seasoning. Cooking the liquid, butter, and flour on the stovetop results in a very thick dough, which is then cooled in a mixer before eggs are added. It is important to add the eggs slowly once the dough has cooled to 140°F or below. If the eggs are added too quickly, or all at once, the final batter will be very thin, will spread excessively when piped or spooned out, and will not rise properly. If the dough is too hot before the eggs are added, the final batter may not expand completely in the oven because the eggs will partially cook in the hot dough prior to reaching the oven. Take a good look at the batter after all the eggs are added. It should be thick enough to pipe from a piping bag without a struggle, have a shiny appearance, and fall from a spoon or rubber spatula slowly and in a thick stream. Baked choux paste will look golden brown and will have doubled from its original size.

PIE DOUGH

The mixing method and the flaky baked texture of pie dough are very different from that of short dough. First the butter is combined with flour. The incorporation of the butter is best done with your fingertips or with a food processor. The size of the fat particles when mixed into the flour determines how flaky the dough is going to be once it has been baked. The acceptable size of fat particles for a flaky pie dough can range from half-walnut size to pea-size. Larger fat particles equate to flakier baked pastry. A small amount of ice-cold water is added to the flour-fat mixture to bind the dough together. Unlike savory short dough, flaky pie dough rarely contains flavorings other than salt, making it versatile for sweet or savory double-crust pies, deep-dish pies, potpies, and turnovers.

PUFF DOUGH

Unlike short dough and pie dough, which call for mixing fat and flour together into small particles, classic puff dough starts with a flour/water dough that is rolled into a rectangle. Cold butter is spread on the dough's surface. It is then folded and rolled as many as eight times before using. The process of making puff dough is time-consuming, yet it is well worth the end result of a flaky, crisp, and flavorful pastry. Puff pastry dough usually does not contain flavorings other than salt, and it is utilized in sweet and savory applications.

"Blitz" or "quick" puff pastry is less intimidating to the home baker, and it is usually made in a quarter of the time. Chunks of butter about 1 inch in size are tossed together with the flour in a bowl. Water is briefly stirred into the mixture; then the shaggy mass is poured out onto a work surface, pressed together into a rough rectangle, and rolled and layered four to five times. The combination of large butter chunks and the rolling and layering process helps to create a very flaky baked pastry. Although blitz puff pastry will not rise quite as high as classic puff pastry, it is a favorable alternative with excellent results, plus it saves you time in the kitchen.

QUICK BREADS

Biscuits, cobbler toppings, crêpes, muffins, pancakes, popovers, scones, shortcakes, and waffles all make up the category of quick breads. Dough mixtures for quick breads are generally of two types. The soft dough varieties are usually patted or rolled out and cut into desired shapes. The batter varieties may be "pour" batters, thin enough to be poured, or "drop" batters that are thick enough to be dropped from a spoon.

The correct balance of ingredients, plus mixing as little as possible, are important for most quick breads, with tenderness and moistness being the goals. The mixing of most batters or doughs should be done quickly and briefly. Blending only until the dry ingredients are moistened is key for making a tender product. Overmixing forms gluten and ultimately toughness in a baked good. Breaking a baked, over-mixed muffin in half will show large, elongated holes inside, called tunneling. Poorly balanced ingredients will cause scones, biscuits, and muffins to have a dry taste. Other than butter's ability to tenderize a baked good, liquids such as milk, buttermilk, sour cream, heavy cream, and crème fraîche, play a key role in tenderizing and moistening a baked good.

Chemical leavening agents help to make quick breads light and tender. Soft doughs for biscuits are often lightly kneaded to help develop flakiness, but they are not kneaded enough to toughen the dough. Some loaf breads and muffins are mixed using the "creaming method," which means creaming fat and sugar together first. The texture is much like a moist cake. Recipes in this book do not use the "creaming method" of mixing since sugar is only used sparingly and as a seasoning, rather than used in a key role for sweetening and tenderizing.

SHORT DOUGH

These doughs are made with butter, which gives them the best taste after they are baked. They are generally enriched with eggs and sugar. The category includes tart-type doughs interchangeable as rolled-type cookies. Sweet short dough, also called "pâte sucrée," is usually mixed by blending butter and sugar in a stand mixer or food processor. Eggs are added, and then the dry ingredients are mixed until a dough starts to form. When baked, the dough has the texture of a cookie dough, rich and somewhat sandy.

Most of the savory short dough recipes in this book require a different mixing technique since they do not contain sugar. Creaming butter without sugar can result in a very crumbly baked pastry that feels pasty in the mouth. Therefore, I have found the mixing technique with the best results calls for putting flour (and other flavorings, if desired) in a bowl, and then rubbing the butter into the flour with your fin-gertips or pulsing it in a food processor fitted with a blade attachment until the mixture resembles coarse bread crumbs. Lightly stirring eggs and water into the flour/butter mixture adds moisture and brings the dough together into a mass. Savory short dough can be flavored by adding ingredients such as cheese, garlic, ground nuts, seeds, and a variety of herbs and spices.

SOUFFLÉS

It is important to gently but quickly fold the whipped egg whites into the base for good baking results. Overfolded whipped egg whites will quickly deflate a light soufflé and result in partial puffing when baked. Underfolded whipped egg whites will leave streaks of white marbled throughout the soufflé after it is baked.

WORKING WITH SHORT DOUGH PASTRY, PUFF PASTRY, AND PIE PASTRY

Sometimes working with pastry dough can seem to be a daunting physical activity and challenging mental task. Understanding the feel of a dough, knowing how much and how thin to roll it, or just overcoming personal fears of defeat from working unsuccessfully with flaky pastry in the past can steer you away from the pleasure of success. Don't give up; practice and try these simple techniques to help you succeed in working with dough after you have made it.

If you have never rolled dough before, try several different rolling pins and choose the one you feel most comfortable with.

Roll across the surface with even pressure. This is a biggie! It's easy to roll dough unevenly, one side thick and one side thin, without paying much attention. Practice by feeling the dough around the entire perimeter as you roll and get a feel for its thickness.

Soften refrigerated dough slightly by putting it on your countertop for 10 to 15 minutes. This will help prevent the dough from cracking when it's being rolled, and it keeps you from being tempted to pound it excessively, which would result in delicate layers being pressed together.

Cold short dough will crack less if you knead it slightly after you remove it from the refrigerator. Knead on a lightly floured work surface until it feels like cold and firm like Play-Doh.

Thinly rolled short dough and pie dough can be fragile. Lifting and placing it into a tart pan or pie pan in one piece may seem impossible at times. After rolling short dough to the proper thickness, dust flour on a rimless baking sheet and slide it under the dough. Angle the baking sheet over the tart pan, letting it slide on top of the pan. Press the dough into the bottom and sides carefully.

Brush excess flour off all pastry dough after you have finished rolling it. Excess flour remains on the surface of the dough and bakes, leaving the finished pastry with a burnt, floury taste.

Roll puff dough to the desired thickness and then cut it into shapes using a small, sharp knife. This allows the puff to rise evenly and to its potential. Egg wash only tops of cut-out puff pastry dough. Any egg that drips down the side will also prevent the dough from fully rising.

MUFFINS

SCONES

BISCUITS

PANCAKES

CRÊPES

WAFFLES

LOAVES

QUICK BREADS

Tender drop biscuits with delicate poached eggs perched on top. Scones creatively filled with creamy cheese and sweet onions. Fluffy pancakes with an endless variety of flavor combinations and toppings. Crêpes, the thin version of a pancake and a staple food in Paris. All of these have two things in common: These doughs and batters can be made quickly, and they are leavened with baking powder, baking soda, or eggs.

Quick-bread batters range from pourable to thick and spoonable to stiff enough to cut. Some quick breads are baked in muffin cups or loaf or Bundt pans, while others are baked free-form. They are versatile enough to blend extremely well with cinnamon and sugar or savory herbs and cheese. One thing is for sure: Quick breads should be tender and moist.

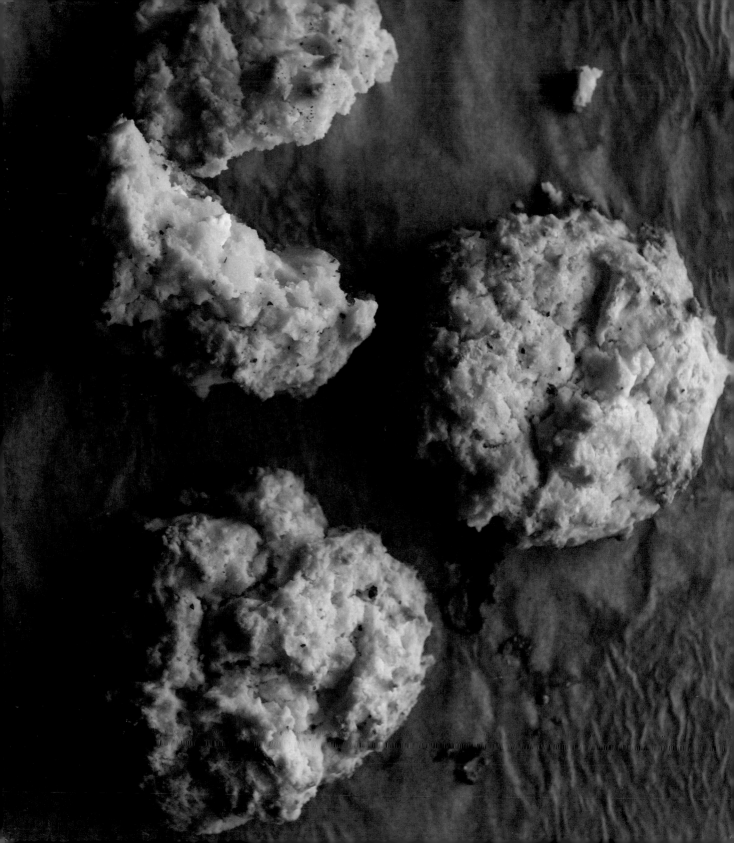

PEPPERED PEAR AND GOAT CHEESE SCONES

Yogurt blended with tangy goat cheese and sweet pears makes for exceptional scones that keep moist for several days. Juicy pears add their own special sweet flavor and moisture to these scones. To accelerate ripening of firm pears, place them in a brown paper bag for a day or two, and they'll quickly undergo a noticeable change in ripeness.

2 CUPS ALL-PURPOSE FLOUR

1½ TEASPOONS BAKING POWDER

2 TABLESPOONS GRANULATED SUGAR

1¼ TEASPOONS SALT

1¼ TEASPOONS FRESHLY CRACKED BLACK PEPPER

½ CUP (1 STICK) UNSALTED BUTTER, COLD AND CUT INTO ½-INCH CUBES

1 MEDIUM PEAR, PEELED, CORED, AND ROUGHLY CHOPPED

4 OUNCES GOAT CHEESE, BROKEN INTO LARGE WALNUT-SIZE PIECES

½ CUP WHOLE OR LOW-FAT (1% OR 2%) PLAIN YOGURT

2 TABLESPOONS WHOLE MILK, PLUS MORE FOR BRUSHING

PREHEAT THE OVEN to 375°F and line a baking sheet with parchment paper or a nonstick baking mat. Put the flour, baking powder, sugar, salt, and pepper in a medium bowl and stir together. Add the butter and break it into pea-size pieces with your fingertips. Sprinkle the pear pieces and crumbled goat cheese over the top of the flour mixture and gently toss together, being careful not to break the cheese into smaller pieces.

SOFTEN THE YOGURT by whisking in the milk. Pour the yogurt over the flour mixture and gently blend the ingredients together with a spatula, being careful not to break up the cheese. The dough may look slightly dry, but it will produce a moist scone. Divide the dough into six equal mounds on the baking sheet, leaving about a 1-inch space between each to allow for slight spreading.

BRUSH THE TOPS of the scones with a little milk. Place the baking pan in the center of the oven and bake until lightly brown, about 25 minutes. Remove the baking sheet from the oven to a cooling rack. Serve warm or at room temperature.

SCONES STUFFED WITH CARAMELIZED RED ONIONS AND BRIE

Creamy Brie and the sweetness of caramelized onions are locked inside these tender cream scones, which are great served for brunch, as a snack, or as an accompaniment to warm soup. Try Camembert or Cambozola as a pleasing substitute for the Brie.

ONION FILLING

2 MEDIUM RED ONIONS, PEELED, CUT IN HALF, AND CUT INTO ¼-INCH-THICK SLICES

4 TABLESPOONS EXTRA-VIRGIN OLIVE OIL

SALT AND FRESHLY GROUND BLACK PEPPER

3 TABLESPOONS SHERRY WINE VINEGAR

SCONES

3½ CUPS ALL-PURPOSE FLOUR

1 TABLESPOON BAKING POWDER

½ TEASPOON BAKING SODA

½ TEASPOON SALT

2 CUPS PLUS 3 TABLESPOONS HEAVY (WHIPPING) CREAM

8 OUNCES BRIE, CUT INTO ½-INCH PIECES

TO PREPARE THE FILLING, sauté the onions in the oil in a large wide-bottomed skillet over high heat. Season to taste with salt and pepper. Cook the onions for 10 minutes, stirring once or twice for even cooking; they will start to turn translucent and soften. Decrease the heat to medium, add the sherry wine vinegar, and continue cooking for another 5 minutes, stirring occasionally, until the onions are golden brown and very soft, 20 to 25 minutes. Transfer the caramelized onions to a plate to cool.

TO PREPARE THE SCONES, preheat the oven to 375°F and line the bottom of a baking sheet with parchment paper or a nonstick baking mat. Stir the flour, baking powder, baking soda, and salt together in a medium bowl. Pour 2 cups of the heavy cream over the flour mixture. Mix the flour and cream with your fingers, forming a soft, slightly sticky dough. Mix the dough gently and briefly. Don't worry if you see a few dry flour patches.

TURN THE MOIST DOUGH out onto a floured work surface. Divide it into two equal pieces and gently knead together once or twice; then flatten each piece of dough into a ½-inch-thick disc, about 9 inches in diameter. Dot one disc of dough with the Brie and spread the caramelized onions evenly over the top. Place the other disc of dough on top of the onions and gently press down the edges, sealing the two discs together. Lift the sandwiched disc

onto a cutting board. With a long sharp knife, cut the round disc into twelve pie-shaped wedges (see *Note*).

EVENLY SPACE the scones on the prepared baking sheet, leaving about 1 inch between each one to allow for slight spreading. Brush the tops with the remaining 3 tablespoons of cream. Bake until lightly browned, 15 to 20 minutes. Remove the baking sheet from the oven and place on a cooling rack. Serve warm.

NOTE

I like using a sharp chef's knife for cutting the scones. Push down into the scones quickly, rocking the knife back and forth, like cutting wedges of a pizza. Clean the knife between each cut by running it under hot water. This ensures the knife does not stick to the dough and the scones are neat in appearance.

SOUR CREAM AND DILL MUFFINS

Plenty of rich sour cream complements the dill flavor of these aromatic muffins and helps keep them moist. I enjoy the muffins split and placed under the broiler until brown and warm. Then, spread them with soft cream cheese and top with thin slices of tomato and smoked salmon. Finish with a squeeze of fresh lemon. Breakfast is served!

2¼ CUPS ALL-PURPOSE FLOUR

2½ TEASPOONS BAKING POWDER

1 TEASPOON BAKING SODA

1¼ TEASPOONS SALT

½ CUP FINELY CHOPPED FRESH DILL

2 EGGS

4 TABLESPOONS UNSALTED BUTTER, MELTED

1¼ CUPS SOUR CREAM

⅓ CUP WHOLE MILK

DILL SEEDS FOR GARNISH *(optional)*

PREHEAT THE OVEN to 350°F and butter and lightly flour the insides of 8 muffin cups. Put the flour, baking powder, baking soda, and salt in a large bowl and gently stir together. Put the chopped dill, eggs, melted butter, sour cream, and milk in another bowl and whisk. Pour the dill mixture over the flour mixture and gently blend together to form a soft dough.

DIVIDE THE BATTER evenly between each muffin cup and sprinkle the tops with a few dill seeds, if desired. Bake until the tops spring back when gently touched in the center, 20 to 25 minutes. Remove the pan from the oven and place on a cooling rack. When the muffins are cool, turn the pan upside down and tap the corner of the pan on the countertop to release each muffin. These muffins will last for up to 1 week if well wrapped and stored in an airtight container, then refrigerated as soon as they are cool.

SHARP CHEDDAR AND CHERRY MUFFINS

Cheddar muffins with chewy, tart red cherries are great served warm right out of the oven. For a mouth-watering breakfast or brunch for French-toast lovers, see the Note.

1 CUP DRIED CHERRIES

2 CUPS ALL-PURPOSE FLOUR

2 CUPS (8 OUNCES) FINELY GRATED EXTRA-SHARP CHEDDAR
CHEESE *(see page 24)*

1 TABLESPOON GRANULATED SUGAR

1 TABLESPOON BAKING POWDER

1 TEASPOON SALT

1 CUP WHOLE MILK

2 EGGS

¼ CUP CANOLA OR VEGETABLE OIL

PREHEAT THE OVEN to 350°F and butter and lightly flour the inside of 8 muffin cups. Put the cherries in a small bowl and pour enough hot water over them to cover the tops. Set aside for 10 minutes; then drain.

PUT THE FLOUR, cheese, sugar, baking powder, and salt in a medium bowl and gently stir just to blend the ingredients. Whisk the cherries, milk, eggs, and oil together in a small bowl. Pour the milk mixture over the flour mixture and stir together just until a soft, wet dough forms.

SPOON THE DOUGH evenly into each muffin cup. Bake until the tops are lightly browned and spring back when gently touched in the center, about 20 minutes. Remove the pan from the oven and place on a cooling rack.

WHEN THE MUFFINS are cool, turn the pan upside down and tap the corner of the pan on the countertop to release each muffin. Store in an airtight container at room temperature for up to 3 days, or refrigerate for 4 to 5 days. Warm the muffins by placing them in a preheated 300°F oven for about 5 minutes or splitting them in half and putting them under a broiler until lightly browned.

NOTE

To make tasty Cheddar and Cherry French Toast, butter and lightly flour an 8-by-3-inch loaf pan. Pour the muffin batter into the pan and bake at 375°F for 40 to 45 minutes. Let the bread cool, then cut it into ½-inch-thick slices; dip both sides in a mixture of 3 eggs whisked with ½ cup of milk or half-and-half along with your favorite seasonings.

Preheat and lightly butter or oil a 12- or 14-inch heavy skillet, or lightly butter an electric griddle and set the temperature at 350°F. Grill each side of the French toast until golden brown, about 2 minutes for each side.

HAM-STUDDED DROP BISCUITS WITH POACHED EGGS AND CLASSIC HOLLANDAISE

Bake some of these fluffy buttermilk biscuits loaded with chunks of smoked ham and see how they transform into a stellar meal with the creamy hollandaise and soft-poached eggs. To save time, bake the biscuits ahead and warm them in a 325°F oven for a few minutes just before serving. For another pleasing quick meal, spread the split biscuits with mustard, top with Cheddar cheese, and broil open-faced.

BISCUITS

CORNMEAL

1 CUP ALL-PURPOSE FLOUR

¼ TEASPOON SALT

1 TEASPOON BAKING POWDER

¼ CUP (½ STICK) UNSALTED BUTTER, COLD AND CUT INTO ½-INCH CUBES

4 OUNCES SMOKED HAM, CUT INTO ½-INCH CUBES (*see* Note)

½ CUP BUTTERMILK

HOLLANDAISE SAUCE

3 EGG YOLKS

3 TABLESPOONS WATER

1 CUP CLARIFIED BUTTER, WARM (*see* Note)

1 TEASPOON FRESH LEMON JUICE

SALT AND FRESHLY GROUND WHITE PEPPER

POACHED EGGS

PINCH OF SALT

1 TEASPOON WHITE VINEGAR

8 EGGS

TO PREPARE THE BISCUITS, preheat the oven to 375°F and generously sprinkle cornmeal on a baking sheet. Put the flour, salt, and baking powder in a large bowl and stir just to blend. Add the butter and work it into the flour mixture with your fingertips until the mixture resembles coarse meal; add the ham and distribute evenly into the flour.

POUR THE BUTTERMILK over the dry ingredients and stir gently with a large spoon just until the mixture comes together. The mixture will be soft and sticky. Drop the dough by large tablespoonfuls into 4 mounds on the baking sheet. Bake the biscuits until lightly browned and the tops spring back when gently touched in the center, 25 to 30 minutes. Remove from the oven and set aside.

TO PREPARE THE HOLLANDAISE SAUCE, bring 2 inches of water just to a simmer in a medium saucepan. Combine the egg yolks and water in a small bowl and set the bowl over (but not touching) the saucepan to create a double boiler. Briskly whisk the egg yolks over very low heat until the mixture is thick and white, 2 to 3 minutes.

Remove the bowl from the heat and very slowly drizzle in the warm clarified butter, whisking constantly to emulsify. While whisking, return the bowl to the saucepan to keep the sauce warm, but never allow it to become too hot; the sauce should always be about body temperature. If the sauce appears overly thick while you are adding the butter, thin it with a dash of lemon juice or water. Season to taste with lemon juice, salt, and pepper. Keep the hollandaise in a warm place while poaching the eggs. (This delicate egg sauce has a short shelf life and cannot be kept too long or at too high a temperature.)

TO PREPARE THE POACHED EGGS, bring 2 inches of water to a simmer in a large nonstick sauté pan or skillet over medium heat. Add a pinch of salt and the vinegar. When the bottom of the pan is coated with small bubbles, crack the eggs and place them gently into the water. Increase the heat slightly but don't let the water boil. Let the eggs set for 2 minutes and then, using a flat spatula, gently dislodge the eggs from the bottom of the pan, allowing them to float. For soft-poached eggs, poach them for about 4 minutes (see *Note*).

WHILE THE EGGS ARE POACHING, slice each warm biscuit in half and place 2 halves on each serving plate.

Remove the eggs from the water using a slotted spoon and top each biscuit half with a poached egg. Sprinkle with salt and pepper, and then cover each egg with 1 to 2 tablespoons of hollandaise. Serve while hot.

NOTE

Ask your grocer's deli department to slice a ¼-pound chunk of ham for you. At home, cut it into ½-inch cubes.

For about 1 cup of clarified butter, melt 3 sticks of unsalted butter in a heavy saucepan over low heat until the butter comes to a simmer. Skim the foam from the top and slowly pour the butter into a measuring cup, leaving the milky solids in the bottom of the pan. Discard the milky solids. Three sticks (1½ cups) of butter will yield about 1 cup of clarified butter.

When preparing poached eggs for a crowd, poach them ahead of time, or even the night before, and keep them in a bowl of ice water stored in the refrigerator. To reheat, spoon each egg gently into a pot of simmering water and let them warm for a minute.

POTATO AND SCALLION BUTTER BISCUITS

The addition of cooked potatoes makes a fluffy textured biscuit. Scallions add a delicate subtle springtime flavor. Make a double batch and pile them high in a basket to serve at your next barbecue; they are great with grilled pork tenderloin or beef.

1 SMALL BAKING POTATO, PEELED AND CUT INTO CHUNKS

2 CUPS ALL-PURPOSE FLOUR, PLUS MORE FOR DUSTING *(optional)*

1½ TEASPOONS BAKING POWDER

¼ TEASPOON BAKING SODA

2¼ TEASPOONS SALT

½ CUP (1 STICK) UNSALTED BUTTER, COLD AND CUT INTO ½-INCH CUBES

½ CUP CHOPPED SCALLIONS, GREEN PART ONLY

1 EGG YOLK

3 TABLESPOONS SOUR CREAM

¾ CUP WHOLE MILK

PREHEAT THE OVEN to 375°F and line a baking sheet with parchment paper or a nonstick baking mat. Cook the potatoes in boiling water until fork tender. Drain the water and cool the potatoes. Press the potato chunks through a ricer (see page 24). You should have at least 1 cup of riced potatoes. Set aside.

PUT THE FLOUR, baking powder, baking soda, and salt in a medium bowl and stir together. Add the butter and break it into pea-size pieces with your fingertips. Whisk 1 cup of the riced potatoes with the scallions, egg yolk, sour cream, and milk in a medium bowl. Pour the potato mixture over the flour mixture and gently stir the ingredients together. Don't worry about getting everything completely moistened.

TURN THE DOUGH out onto a floured surface and pat into a 5-by-8-inch rectangle, about 1 inch thick. Cut out 6 biscuits using a 2½-inch round cookie cutter. Place the biscuits on the baking sheet, evenly spaced apart. Dust the tops with a little flour, if desired. Bake until very lightly browned, 18 to 20 minutes. Remove the baking sheet from the oven and serve the biscuits warm.

WHITE CHEDDAR-ZUCCHINI PANCAKES

Delicate zucchini and Cheddar cheese team up to make these extra-moist vegetable pancakes in just minutes. They are delicious served as a side dish with roasted pork and Apple, Pear, and Ginger Chutney (page 142) or just complemented with a dollop of sour cream or Crème Fraîche (page 149). The batter can be made a day in advance and stored airtight in the refrigerator.

2 LARGE EGGS

1 CUP WHOLE MILK

2 TABLESPOONS EXTRA-VIRGIN OLIVE OIL

1½ TEASPOONS SALT

½ TEASPOON GRANULATED SUGAR

1¼ CUPS GRATED FRESH ZUCCHINI, WELL DRAINED *(see* Note)

1¼ CUPS FRESHLY GRATED SHARP WHITE CHEDDAR CHEESE *(see page 24)*

¾ CUP ALL-PURPOSE FLOUR

¾ TEASPOON BAKING POWDER

CRACK THE EGGS into a medium bowl and whisk in the milk, olive oil, salt, and sugar. Add the zucchini and cheese. Put the flour and baking powder in a large bowl and stir together. Pour the flour mixture over the zucchini mixture and whisk the batter smooth.

PREHEAT AND OIL OR BUTTER a 12- or 14-inch heavy skillet, or lightly oil an electric griddle and set it at 350°F. Drop ¼ cupfuls of batter into the skillet. Cook the pancake on one side until the edges begin to look puffed and bubbles form and start to break. Turn the pancake over, cooking until brown and firm, about 1 minute more. Serve hot.

NOTE

The best-flavored zucchini are small, firm, and young, between 5 and 7 inches long. They can be purchased in late spring through summer. Skins should be tender and thin, puncturing easily with a fingernail. To drain the grated zucchini, place it on top of two paper towels. Lay two more paper towels on top of the zucchini and gently press out the excess moisture.

BUCKWHEAT BLINIS WITH WARM BING CHERRIES AND CRÈME FRAÎCHE

Everything in this recipe can be made ahead of time (see Note). Then it takes just a few minutes to bake and assemble the delicious classic buckwheat pancakes oozing with thyme-scented cherries. Enjoy these mouthwatering sweet and savory pancakes as an appetizer, at a cocktail party, or for brunch.

3 EGGS

¾ CUP BUTTERMILK

I CUP WHOLE MILK

6 TABLESPOONS UNSALTED BUTTER, MELTED

I TEASPOON GRATED LEMON ZEST

I CUP ALL-PURPOSE FLOUR

¾ CUP BUCKWHEAT FLOUR

¼ TEASPOON SALT

I RECIPE WARM BING CHERRIES *(page 148)*

½ CUP CRÈME FRAÎCHE *(page 149)*

WHISK THE EGGS, buttermilk, milk, butter, and lemon zest together in a medium bowl. Add the all-purpose flour, buckwheat flour, and salt. Whisk until smooth.

PLACE A SAUTÉ PAN OR SKILLET over medium heat and spray it lightly with cooking oil. Spoon tablespoon-size dollops of batter into the pan, leaving space for them to spread a little. Cook until bubbles appear on the surface of each blini, about 1 minute; flip them over and cook the other side for another minute. Place the pancakes on a baking sheet and continue until all of the blinis are cooked.

TOP EACH BLINI with a teaspoon of Warm Bing Cherries and a ½ teaspoon of Crème Fraîche. Serve warm or at room temperature.

NOTE

The blini batter can be made ahead and stored in the refrigerator for up to 2 days. The cherries and Crème Fraîche can also be made ahead, stored in airtight containers, and refrigerated for up to 1 week.

SHALLOT CRÊPE ROLLUPS FILLED WITH FRESH CARROT-GINGER SALAD

Serve this dish chilled on a hot summer day. Light, cool, and crunchy carrot salad accented with a hint of sweetness and an Asian flair hides inside these delicate crêpes. Make the crêpes a day ahead and roll them up quickly to serve as an appetizer, a first course, or a side dish, or enjoy two for a light summer entrée.

CRÊPES

¾ CUP ALL-PURPOSE FLOUR

1 TEASPOON GRANULATED SUGAR

½ TEASPOON SALT

2 EGGS

¾ CUP WHOLE OR LOW-FAT MILK

3 TABLESPOONS FINELY MINCED SHALLOTS

CARROT SALAD FILLING

1 LARGE CARROT, GRATED, ABOUT 1¼ CUPS (*see* Note)

½ CUP CRÈME FRAÎCHE (*page 149*) OR SOUR CREAM, PLUS MORE FOR GARNISH

½ CUP GOLDEN RAISINS

5 TABLESPOONS PICKLED GINGER, DRAINED AND ROUGHLY CHOPPED, PLUS MORE FOR GARNISH

2 TABLESPOONS GRATED ORANGE ZEST

2 TEASPOONS SESAME OIL

½ TEASPOON SALT

FRESH CHIVES FOR GARNISH (*optional*)

TO PREPARE THE CRÊPES, stir the flour, sugar, and salt together in a small bowl. Put the eggs and milk in a blender and mix for a few seconds. Add the flour mixture and blend until completely smooth, about 15 seconds. Strain the batter through a fine-mesh strainer. Gently stir in the shallots. Let the batter rest for half an hour before cooking.

LINE A TRAY with parchment paper. Heat a crêpe pan or a 7-inch nonstick sauté pan or skillet over moderately high heat. Spray the pan lightly with cooking oil or brush with melted butter. Pour ¼ cup of the batter into the sides of the pan and swirl to coat the bottom, forming a thin layer. Cook until bubbles appear on the surface of the crêpe and the edges begin to brown lightly. Flip the crêpe over using a spatula. Cook the second side for about 10 seconds, then turn the crêpe onto the prepared tray to cool. Continue cooking crêpes until all the batter is used. You should have 6 crêpes.

TO PREPARE THE FILLING, stir all of the ingredients together in a medium bowl. Lay the crêpes on a clean work surface. Spoon the carrot filling just left of the center on all 6 crêpes, dividing the mixture equally. Roll up each crêpe starting on the left side. Place the crêpes on a serving platter and garnish with a teaspoon of Crème Fraîche, chopped pickled ginger, and a small piece of chive, if desired.

NOTE

I like the delicate sweetness of organic carrots for this dish. The quickest way to grate carrots is with a medium grater blade attachment of a food processor. A fine grater blade will produce finely shredded carrots that have a tendency to become soggy and lack crunchiness. Store any remaining crêpe rollups wrapped and refrigerated for up to 2 days.

HAZELNUT WAFFLES

I have never forgotten the hazelnut waffle I ordered at a family-style restaurant years ago. Then, and still now, I remember the waffle's delicate, nutty flavor. Try this dish for lunch or brunch. For a fun breakfast waffle idea, try serving each waffle with Warm Bing Cherries (page 148) or apple compote and maple butter.

⅓ CUP HAZELNUTS, TOASTED AND GROUND (*see* Note)

1¼ CUPS ALL-PURPOSE FLOUR

1 TABLESPOON GRANULATED SUGAR

1½ TEASPOONS BAKING POWDER

½ TEASPOON SALT

2 EGGS

1 CUP WHOLE MILK

¼ CUP (½ STICK) UNSALTED BUTTER, MELTED

TO PREPARE THE WAFFLES, combine the ground hazelnuts, flour, sugar, baking powder, and salt together in a medium bowl. Gently whisk the eggs, milk, and melted butter together in another bowl. Pour the liquid ingredients over the dry ingredients and whisk until smooth, about 30 seconds. Set the waffle batter aside.

PREHEAT THE OVEN to 325°F. Preheat the waffle iron to medium-high or according to the manufacturer's instructions. Brush the waffle-iron grids with a little oil or melted butter. For each waffle, pour about ¹/₃ cup batter onto the grid. Close the lid and bake until the waffle is crisp and well browned, about 4 minutes. Remove the waffle and place on the baking sheet. Put the baking sheet into the oven to keep the waffles warm as you work. Continue until all 6 waffles are made.

PLACE EACH WAFFLE on a warm serving plate. Spoon or ladle a good ¹/₃ cup of apple compote or Warm Bing Cherries over each waffle. Serve warm.

NOTE

Since hazelnuts are usually covered with a thin, clingy brown skin, they require special care after toasting and before grinding. Once the nuts are toasted (see page 25), the skins will loosen a bit from the nut. Wrap the warm, toasted nuts in a clean dish towel and rub vigorously to remove most of their skins. Alternatively, the nuts can be put in a medium-mesh strainer and rubbed against the mesh to loosen the skins. Don't worry if all the skin does not release from the nuts. Remove as much as possible and then pick the nuts out and proceed to grind.

For finely ground nuts, place them in the bowl of a food processor fitted with a blade attachment and pulse until fine.

PUMPKIN-HAZELNUT SPICE LOAF

This unusual savory loaf is packed with moistness and lots of spices, nuts, and fruit. Enjoy thick slices with hearty bowls of soup on cool fall days.

¾ CUP RAISINS

¾ CUP WHOLE-WHEAT FLOUR

¾ CUP ALL-PURPOSE FLOUR

2 TABLESPOONS LIGHTLY PACKED LIGHT BROWN SUGAR

¾ TEASPOON BAKING POWDER

½ TEASPOON BAKING SODA

½ TEASPOON SALT

2 TEASPOONS GROUND CINNAMON

¾ TEASPOON GROUND GINGER

¼ TEASPOON GROUND NUTMEG

¼ TEASPOON GROUND ALLSPICE

¼ TEASPOON GROUND CLOVES

¼ TEASPOON DRIED SAGE

½ CUP FINELY GRATED SHARP CHEDDAR CHEESE *(see page 24)*

¾ CUP PUMPKIN PURÉE

½ CUP VEGETABLE OIL

½ CUP (2 OUNCES) CHOPPED HAZELNUTS

2 EGGS

2 TABLESPOONS WHOLE MILK

PREHEAT THE OVEN to 350°F. Lightly oil an 8-by-3-inch loaf pan and dust with flour. Put the raisins in a small bowl and pour enough hot water over them to cover the tops. Set aside for 10 minutes and then drain.

SIFT THE WHOLE-WHEAT FLOUR, all-purpose flour, brown sugar, baking powder, baking soda, salt, cinnamon, ginger, nutmeg, allspice, cloves, and sage together into a large bowl. Put the drained raisins, Cheddar cheese, pumpkin purée, oil, hazelnuts, eggs, and milk in a medium bowl and whisk to combine. Pour the pumpkin mixture over the flour mixture and gently blend with a rubber spatula. Spoon the batter evenly into the prepared loaf pan. Bake until the top springs back when gently touched in the center, 45 to 55 minutes. Remove the pan from the oven and place on a cooling rack for 10 minutes. Turn the loaf pan over and gently tap on the counter to release the bread. Serve the bread warm or let cool completely before wrapping airtight in plastic film. Store at room temperature for up to 1 week.

BUTTERMILK TARRAGON LOAF

A tiny bit of sugar brings out the sweetness of the tarragon in this herb-scented quick bread. Toast thick slices and serve open-faced slathered with whole-grain mustard, or butter the slices and layer with warm roast chicken breast, thin apple slices, Brie, and fresh arugula. Drizzle with lemon-scented olive oil, and you're ready for a blissful lunch.

1 LARGE CLOVE GARLIC, MINCED

4 TABLESPOONS UNSALTED BUTTER

1¾ CUPS ALL-PURPOSE FLOUR

2 TEASPOONS BAKING POWDER

1 TEASPOON SALT

1 TEASPOON FRESHLY GROUND BLACK PEPPER

1 TABLESPOON GRANULATED SUGAR

1 TABLESPOON FINELY CHOPPED FRESH TARRAGON

1 EGG

¼ CUP SOUR CREAM

1 CUP BUTTERMILK

PREHEAT THE OVEN to 350°F and butter or spray an 8-by-3-inch loaf pan. Put the garlic and butter in a small saucepan over medium heat just long enough to melt the butter. Set aside.

STIR THE FLOUR, baking powder, salt, pepper, sugar, and tarragon together in a medium bowl. Crack the egg into a small bowl and whisk in the sour cream and buttermilk. Pour the egg mixture and garlic butter over the flour mixture and stir just to moisten the dry ingredients; don't worry about a few dry spots in the dough.

Spoon the dough into the prepared pan and place it in the oven. Bake until the top springs back when gently touched in the center, 45 to 55 minutes. Put the loaf on a cooling rack until just warm. Unmold the loaf and wrap it in plastic film. This bread will stay moist and flavorful at room temperature for up to 1 week.

SMOKED-SALMON CRÊPE TORTE

Layers and layers of thin, tender whole-wheat crêpes and smoked salmon make a stunning multilayered cakelike torte. To serve, cut into small wedges for an appetizer or into slightly larger wedges to accompany a salad.

CRÊPES

½ CUP WHOLE-WHEAT FLOUR

½ CUP ALL-PURPOSE FLOUR

¼ TEASPOON SALT

1¼ CUPS WHOLE MILK

2 EGGS

2 TABLESPOONS UNSALTED BUTTER, MELTED

SMOKED-SALMON FILLING

ONE 8-OUNCE PACKAGE CREAM CHEESE AT ROOM TEMPERATURE

1 TABLESPOON PLUS 2 TEASPOONS ROUGHLY CHOPPED SCALLION, GREEN PART ONLY

2 TEASPOONS CAPERS, DRAINED AND RINSED

½ TEASPOON FRESH LEMON JUICE

2 TABLESPOONS WHOLE MILK

ONE 4-OUNCE PACKAGE SMOKED SALMON

TO PREPARE THE CRÊPES, stir the whole-wheat flour, all-purpose flour, and salt together in a medium bowl. Whisk the milk, eggs, and melted butter together in a small bowl. Pour half of the milk mixture into the flour mixture and whisk until smooth. Add the remaining milk mixture and continue whisking until the batter is completely smooth. Strain the batter through a fine-mesh strainer. Let the batter rest for half an hour before cooking.

LINE A TRAY with parchment paper. Heat a crêpe pan or a 7-inch nonstick sauté pan or skillet over moderately high heat. Spray the pan lightly with cooking oil or brush with melted butter. Pour ¼ cup of batter into the side of the pan and swirl to coat the bottom, forming a thin layer. Cook until bubbles appear on the surface of the crêpe and the edges begin to brown lightly. Flip the crêpe over using a spatula. Cook the second side for about 10 seconds, then turn the crêpe onto the prepared tray to cool. Continue cooking crêpes until all the batter is used. You should have 11 crêpes (*see* Note).

TO PREPARE THE FILLING, in the bowl of a food processor fitted with a blade attachment, process the cream cheese until smooth, about 30 seconds. Scrape the bowl with a rubber spatula and add the scallion, capers, lemon juice, milk, and salmon. Process for another 15 seconds,

CONTINUED ➤

then scrape the bowl with a rubber spatula again. Blend for another 10 seconds or until the mixture looks fairly smooth. Divide the filling into 10 portions, each about 2 heaping tablespoons.

PLACE A CRÊPE on a serving plate and spread one portion of filling completely and evenly over its surface with a metal offset spatula or the back of a spoon. Top with another crêpe and carefully spread another portion of filling on top, making sure you spread to the edges. Continue until all of the filling and the crêpes are stacked, ending with a plain crêpe on top. Cover the torte with plastic film and chill for at least half an hour before slicing and serving.

CUT THE TORTE into small wedges with a sharp knife. Clean the knife between cuts to make a neat sliced appearance. Any remaining pieces of torte can be wrapped tightly with plastic film and stored in the refrigerator for up to 1 week.

NOTE

The crêpes and the filling can be made a day ahead and refrigerated. Let the filling come to room temperature and assemble as directed.

CHILE-CHEESE GRATIN SANDWICHES

MAKES

8

SERVINGS

Thick slices of warm, moist cheese bread with a kick of jalapeño are topped with ripe tomato slices and a cheese topping, then broiled until bubbly and golden brown. Make the bread and topping ahead and toast sandwiches in an instant. You'll be sure to make these fork and knife open-faced sandwiches often for lunch or brunch.

CHILE-CHEESE BREAD

2 CUPS ALL-PURPOSE FLOUR

2 TEASPOONS GRANULATED SUGAR

I TABLESPOON BAKING POWDER

I TEASPOON FRESHLY GROUND BLACK PEPPER

I TEASPOON SALT

4 OUNCES (I CUP) SHARP CHEDDAR CHEESE, SHREDDED *(see page 24)*

I CUP WHOLE MILK

⅓ CUP VEGETABLE OIL

I EGG

ONE 4-OUNCE CAN PEELED MILD GREEN CHILES, DRAINED

3 TABLESPOONS FINELY CHOPPED JALAPEÑO CHILE, VEINED AND SEEDED

½ CUP FINELY CHOPPED RED BELL PEPPER

CHEDDAR TOPPING

4 OUNCES (I STICK) UNSALTED BUTTER AT ROOM TEMPERATURE

4 OUNCES (I CUP) SHARP CHEDDAR CHEESE, SHREDDED *(see page 24)*

I OUNCE (¼ CUP) ROMANO CHEESE, SHREDDED

½ TEASPOON WORCESTERSHIRE SAUCE

¼ TEASPOON GARLIC POWDER

PINCH OF SALT

8 TOMATO SLICES, CUT ¼ INCH THICK

TO PREPARE THE BREAD, preheat the oven to 375°F and butter or spray an 8-by-3-inch loaf pan. Stir the flour, sugar, baking powder, pepper, and salt together in a medium bowl. Add the cheese and gently toss until the cheese is evenly distributed throughout the mixture.

WHISK THE MILK, oil, egg, green chiles, chopped jalapeño, and red bell pepper together in another bowl. Pour the milk mixture over the flour mixture and briefly blend

with a spatula. The batter will look moist. Pour the batter into the prepared pan and place it in the oven. Bake until the top is golden brown and springs back when gently touched in the center, about 45 minutes. Put the loaf on a cooling rack for 10 minutes and then remove the bread from the pan to completely cool (see *Note*).

MEANWHILE, PREPARE THE TOPPING. Put the butter, Cheddar and Romano cheeses, Worcestershire

CONTINUED ➤

sauce, garlic powder, and a little salt in the bowl of a stand mixer fitted with a whip attachment. Whip for 2 minutes on medium speed. Alternatively, the topping can be pulsed in a food processor for about 1 minute (see *Note*).

SET THE OVEN to broil. Cut the loaf into 8 slices and lay the slices on a baking sheet. Place a tomato slice on each piece of bread. Spoon about 2 heaping tablespoons of the cheese topping over each tomato slice. Put the baking sheet into the oven about 4 inches away from the flame and broil until the cheese is bubbly and golden brown, 3 to 5 minutes. Serve immediately.

NOTE

Wrap cooled bread in plastic film and store at room temperature for up to 1 week, or freeze for up to 1 month. Remove the loaf from the freezer and thaw at room temperature for a couple of hours. Warm in a 300°F oven for 15 minutes before serving.

The Cheddar topping can be made ahead and stored in the refrigerator for up to 2 weeks.

SHORT
DOUGH

PUFF
PASTRY
DOUGH

FLAKY
PIE
PASTRY

PHYLLO
DOUGH

FLAKY PASTRIES

When I was growing up, I dreamed of making flaky pastry. I can still taste my favorite potpies and the cherry turnover Mom used to make. I learned the techniques of making pastry dough by practicing. Soon I started to mix, roll, and layer all sorts of flaky dough recipes, and filled or covered them with delicious ingredients. Take time to practice and master the techniques of making your favorite pastry dough for potpies and cherry turnovers.

BAKED POMODORO DUMPLINGS ON AN OLIVE SALAD

A pretty visual presentation and the delicious flavor of warm tomatoes in crunchy phyllo nestled on top of a Greek-influenced olive salad make this perfect for a first course! The preparation for these tomato dumplings is similar to that for sweet dumplings such as apples wrapped in pastry and baked. Flaky phyllo pastry replaces pie pastry and tomatoes replace the apples.

OLIVE SALAD

1 RECIPE TAPENADE CREAM, OMITTING THE CREAM CHEESE *(page 145)*

1 CUP CRUMBLED FETA CHEESE

DUMPLINGS

3 MEDIUM ROMA TOMATOES

SALT AND FRESHLY GROUND BLACK PEPPER

½ POUND (8 OUNCES) PHYLLO PASTRY, THAWED *(see page 15)*

½ CUP EXTRA-VIRGIN OLIVE OIL

2 TEASPOONS DRIED OREGANO

FOR THE OLIVE SALAD, prepare 1 recipe of the Tapenade Cream, omitting the cream cheese and roughly chopping the remaining ingredients. Put the olive salad into a small bowl and toss with ¾ cup of the feta cheese. Set aside.

TO MAKE THE DUMPLINGS, preheat the oven to 375°F. Cut the tomatoes in half lengthwise and season to taste with salt and pepper. Set aside.

UNWRAP AND UNROLL the thawed phyllo dough. Cut it in half with a sharp knife. Stack the cut sheets together and put them on a work surface. Lay a lightly dampened cloth over the top to keep the dough moist as you work.

PUT ONE SHEET OF PHYLLO on a clean surface. Lightly brush it with olive oil and dust with the oregano. Repeat the process with 4 more sheets of phyllo, oil, and

oregano to end up with 5 layers. (You will make six of these layered phyllo stacks.) Lay a tomato half, with the cut side down, on each of the pieces of layered phyllo. Trim the phyllo around the tomato into a circle leaving a 2-inch edge to wrap over the tomato. Pull the phyllo up over the tomato and press the ends together, sealing in the tomato completely. Carefully pick up the wrapped tomato, turn it over, and place it on the baking sheet seam side down. Repeat until all the tomatoes are wrapped in phyllo and place them all on the baking sheet.

LIGHTLY BRUSH THE PHYLLO packages with olive oil and sprinkle with the remaining ¼ cup feta cheese. Transfer the baking sheet to the oven and bake the wrapped tomatoes until golden brown, 25 to 30 minutes. Divide the olive salad among 6 serving plates and top each with a tomato dumpling. Serve warm.

CAESAR TARTLETS WITH SWEET GARLIC-BUTTER CRUSTS

Show your creativity with this showstopper of a first course. Sweet roasted garlic and Parmesan cheese are baked into tender tart shells. Caesar salad is then piled high inside.

GARLIC TARTLETS

2 SMALL WHOLE HEADS OF GARLIC

2 TEASPOONS EXTRA-VIRGIN OLIVE OIL

1 CUP (2 STICKS) UNSALTED BUTTER AT ROOM TEMPERATURE

½ CUP FINELY GRATED PARMESAN CHEESE *(see page 24)*

½ TEASPOON SALT

2½ CUPS ALL-PURPOSE FLOUR

CAESAR VINAIGRETTE & SALAD

1 GARLIC CLOVE, PEELED AND MINCED

1 TABLESPOON CAPERS, RINSED AND CHOPPED

2 TEASPOONS CHOPPED FRESH PARSLEY

1 TEASPOON ANCHOVY PASTE

½ TEASPOON WORCESTERSHIRE SAUCE

1 TABLESPOON PLUS 1 TEASPOON RED WINE VINEGAR

¼ TEASPOON FRESH LEMON JUICE

¼ TEASPOON SALT

PINCH OF CAYENNE PEPPER

¼ CUP EXTRA-VIRGIN OLIVE OIL

¼ CUP FINELY GRATED PARMESAN CHEESE *(see page 24)*

FRESHLY GROUND BLACK PEPPER

1 HEAD OF ROMAINE LETTUCE, LEAVES WASHED AND TORN

TO MAKE THE TARTLETS, preheat the oven to 350°F. Trim the tops off the garlic heads to expose the cloves. Sprinkle with olive oil. Wrap the garlic in aluminum foil and place on a baking sheet. Roast until very soft, about 35 minutes. Let cool and then remove each clove with the tip of a knife.

IN THE BOWL of an electric mixer fitted with a paddle attachment, beat the roasted garlic, butter, cheese, and salt together until smooth, about 1 minute. Add the flour and blend well; the dough will look completely crumbly. Place a generous ¼ cup of the dough mixture into eight 4-inch tartlet pans. Press the dough evenly

and firmly into the bottom and up the sides of the tartlet pans. Place the tarts on a baking sheet and bake until lightly browned, 18 to 20 minutes. Put the baking sheet on a cooling rack and let cool before removing the baked pastry from each mold.

MEANWHILE, prepare the vinaigrette. Put the garlic, capers, parsley, anchovy paste, Worcestershire sauce, red wine vinegar, lemon juice, salt, and cayenne pepper into a medium bowl and whisk to combine. Slowly drizzle in the olive oil while continuously whisking to emulsify the vinaigrette. Stir in the grated cheese and season to taste with pepper (see *Note*).

PUT THE PREPARED GREENS in a large bowl and drizzle with some of the vinaigrette. Toss gently to coat the greens lightly. Add more vinaigrette to taste. Place a heaping portion of greens into each tartlet shell and finish with a grinding of pepper. Serve immediately.

NOTE

The Caesar vinaigrette can be made up to 2 days before serving. Refrigerate and store in an airtight container.

CHILI-GRILLED EGGPLANT AND SWEET ROASTED PEPPER TARTLETS IN POPPY SEED SHELLS

MAKES

4

SERVINGS

Spicy eggplant and sweet peppers are tossed together and piled into toasted poppy seed pastry to make a color-ful first course or a side dish to accompany fish or meat. Prepare the components ahead of time and simply assemble just before serving. For a spicier filling, season the vegetables with more chili oil to your liking.

6 TABLESPOONS POPPY SEEDS

1¼ CUPS ALL-PURPOSE FLOUR

½ TEASPOON SALT

6 TABLESPOONS UNSALTED BUTTER, COLD AND CUT INTO ½-INCH CUBES

1 EGG

2 TEASPOONS COLD WATER

½ RECIPE RICOTTA FILLING AND DIP (*page 147*)

1 RECIPE CHILI-GRILLED EGGPLANT AND SWEET ROASTED PEPPERS, PLUS THE BALSAMIC JULIENNED ROASTED PEPPERS FROM THE SAME RECIPE (*page 153*)

PREHEAT THE OVEN to 350°F. Put four 4-inch tartlet pans on a baking sheet. Combine the poppy seeds, flour, and salt in a medium bowl. Add the butter and work it into the flour mixture with your fingertips until the mix-ture resembles coarse bread crumbs; this can also be done by pulsing ingredients in a food processor as well. Stir in the egg and cold water. Put the dough onto a lightly floured work surface, knead it a couple of times, then form it into a flat disc (see *Note*).

DIVIDE THE DOUGH into 2 pieces. Roll one piece of the dough out with a rolling pin to about ¼ inch thick. Cut the dough to fit 2 of the tartlet pans. Gently press the dough into each pan and trim the pastry flush with the pans to create a neat appearance. Roll the other half of the dough and line the remaining tartlet pans. Place the baking sheet into the oven and bake until light brown, 12 to 15 minutes. Put the tartlets on a cooling rack and let cool before removing the baked crusts from each pan.

PUT EACH TARTLET SHELL on an individual serving plate. Spoon 2 to 3 tablespoons of the Ricotta Filling into the center of each shell. Top with ⅓ cup of Chili-Grilled Eggplant and Sweet Roasted Peppers, mounding it slightly. Garnish with balsamic julienned roasted peppers. Serve the tartlets at room temperature or, if desired, carefully place them on a baking sheet for warming. Heat in a 350°F oven for 10 minutes.

NOTE

The dough can be made ahead of time. To store, flatten it into a disc and wrap the dough in plastic film. Refrigerate for up to 3 days, or freeze for up to 1 month.

CAMBOZOLA PEAR CREAM TART

Ripe pears and the flavor of Cambozola cheese meld together in a delicate, melt-in-your-mouth toasted walnut–crust tart. Most pears will be very firm when purchased from the market and can take up to 2 weeks to soften. To accelerate ripening, place them in a brown paper bag and set them on a countertop for a day or two; they will undergo a noticeable change quickly. Use pears that have a slight yield to pressure and start to become fragrant; they should slice easily. I love this elegant tart served with a small salad as a first course or for a light lunch.

TART DOUGH

½ CUP (1 STICK) UNSALTED BUTTER AT ROOM TEMPERATURE

¾ TEASPOON SALT

1 EGG WHITE

¼ CUP DRY BREAD CRUMBS

1 CUP ALL-PURPOSE FLOUR

1¼ CUPS WALNUT PIECES, TOASTED

FILLING

4 OUNCES CAMBOZOLA CHEESE (*see* Note)

3 EGG YOLKS

¾ CUP PLUS 2 TABLESPOONS HEAVY (WHIPPING) CREAM

½ TEASPOON FRESHLY GROUND BLACK PEPPER

1 MEDIUM PEAR, FIRM BUT RIPE

TO PREPARE THE TART DOUGH, put the butter and salt together in the bowl of a food processor fitted with a blade attachment and process for 30 seconds. Scrape the bowl with a rubber spatula, add the egg white, and process for another 30 seconds. The egg white should be thoroughly emulsified into the butter and look smooth. Add the bread crumbs, flour, and walnut pieces all at once. Pulse until the walnuts are fine and the dough comes together into a ball, about 1 minute. Turn the dough out on a floured surface and knead briefly. Press into a disc about 1 inch thick and wrap in plastic film. Refrigerate for 15 minutes while preparing the filling.

PREHEAT THE OVEN to 350°F and place a 9-inch fluted tart pan with a removable bottom on a flat baking sheet.

PREPARE THE FILLING. Put the cheese, egg yolks, cream, and pepper in the bowl of a food processor. Process until smooth, about 30 seconds. Pour the filling into a container with a spout to make it easy for pouring.

REMOVE THE TART DOUGH from the refrigerator and place on a well-floured surface. Dust the top of the dough generously with flour. Using a rolling pin, carefully roll the dough into a 12-inch circle about $^1/8$ inch thick. Dust more flour under and on top of the dough to keep it from sticking to the surface while rolling, if needed. Slide a flat, rimless baking sheet under the dough and transfer it to the tart pan. Center the dough and press it gently into the bottom and sides of the pan. Patch any tears with dough scraps. Trim the top edge of the crust with your fingers or a small knife. Bake until the crust is medium golden brown, 25 to 30 minutes. Set the pan on a rack to cool.

REDUCE THE OVEN TEMPERATURE to 300°F. Stand the pear upright on a cutting board. With a small paring knife, cut off one side of the pear close to the core. Turn the pear around to the opposite side and cut off the other side. Then cut off the two small sides of the pear and discard the core. Lay the cut sides on the cutting board and cut each piece of pear into ¼-inch slices. Place the slices on the bottom of the baked shell, overlapping them like shingles. Carefully pour the custard over the pears and return the pan to the center of the oven. Bake until the custard is set, about 25 minutes. The top should just start to turn light golden and the filling will jiggle slightly

in the center. Remove it to a rack and let cool slightly. Remove the ring from the tart, transfer to a serving platter, and serve warm or at room temperature. Leftovers can be wrapped in plastic film and refrigerated for up to 3 days. Remove the tart from the refrigerator, place on a baking sheet, and warm for 15 minutes at 300°F

NOTE

Cambozola cheese has a creamy white interior with a white rind. It is a soft-ripened cheese that tastes like a cross between Camembert and Gorgonzola.

ONION AND SHERRY CREAM TURNOVERS

These warm, crunchy, whole-wheat puff-pastry turnovers are oozing with creamed onions accented with sherry. Choose a variety of onions to your liking—from sweet and mild to pungent and robust. I like a combination of Vidalia and cipollini for their sweetness, and yellow globe for its pungent kick.

WHOLE-WHEAT PASTRY

1 CUP ALL-PURPOSE FLOUR

½ CUP WHOLE-WHEAT FLOUR

¾ TEASPOON SALT

¾ CUP (1½ STICKS) UNSALTED BUTTER, COLD AND CUT INTO ½-INCH CUBES

1 CUP COLD WATER

ONION FILLING

3 TABLESPOONS EXTRA-VIRGIN OLIVE OIL

3 SMALL ONIONS, PEELED AND ROUGHLY CHOPPED

½ TEASPOON SALT

1½ CUPS CHICKEN OR VEGETABLE BROTH

½ CUP DRY SHERRY

2 CUPS HEAVY (WHIPPING) CREAM

JAPANESE BREAD CRUMBS (PANKO) FOR GARNISH

COARSE SEA SALT FOR GARNISH

TO PREPARE THE PASTRY, stir the all-purpose flour, whole-wheat flour, and salt together in a medium bowl. Add the butter and toss, being careful not to break the butter into smaller pieces. Drizzle the water over the mixture and blend together with your hands until a shaggy dough forms. The flour will look dry in places and be dotted with chunks of the butter. Turn the dough out onto a floured work surface and knead together once or twice, just until the dough sticks together completely. Pat into a rectangle about 2 inches thick and dust the top of the dough with flour. The dough will still look a bit rough and dry but it will come together nicely once it has been rolled. Roll the dough into a 10-by-15-inch rectangle, about ½ inch thick. Dust the flour off the top

of the dough and fold in half lengthwise. Fold in half again, forming a long, thin rectangle. Turn the dough so the long side is facing you and continue to roll again into another 10-by-15-inch rectangle. Fold again in half. Wrap in plastic film and refrigerate for 15 minutes. Roll out the dough two more times the same as before. Wrap tightly in plastic film and refrigerate (see *Note*).

MEANWHILE, PREPARE THE FILLING. Pour the olive oil into a large wide-bottomed pan and add the onions and salt. Cover with a lid and cook on high for 5 minutes. Stir in the broth and sherry. Reduce the heat to medium-high and cook for 20 minutes, stirring occasionally. Remove the lid and stir in the cream. Cover and cook, stirring occasionally, until the onions are creamy with a soft puddinglike thickness, about 40 minutes. Transfer the onions to a bowl and chill completely before assembling.

PREHEAT THE OVEN to 400°F and fit a baking sheet with parchment paper or a nonstick baking mat. Unwrap the dough and place it on a floured work surface. Roll it into a 10-by-15-inch rectangle. Cut the dough in half lengthwise to make two 5-by-15-inch strips. Cut each strip into thirds to form six 5-by-5-inch squares. Place ¼ cup of the cold onions on the bottom half of each piece of pastry. Moisten the rim of each pastry with a little water. Fold the top half of each pastry over the filling, pressing and sealing gently with your finger around the

rim of the turnover. Press down gently with a fork to make a decorative edge. Make a small slit on top for steam to escape and brush a little water on the turnovers. Sprinkle with the bread crumbs and sea salt. Space the turnovers evenly on the baking sheet. Bake until dark golden brown, about 25 minutes. Transfer to a cooling rack and serve warm or at room temperature.

NOTE

The quick puff pastry can be made, wrapped tightly, and kept in the refrigerator for up to 2 days, or it can be frozen for up to 1 month before using.

SWEET POTATO, GOLDEN RAISIN, AND CRANBERRY STRUDEL

Don't expect to have leftovers of this crunchy strudel. Brown butter and toasted pecans bring a rich buttered nuttiness to the earthy sweet potatoes and chewy dried fruit. Enjoy generous slices for a light lunch or as a side dish with roasted meat. You had better make two!

¼ CUP DRIED CRANBERRIES

¼ CUP GOLDEN RAISINS

1 MEDIUM SWEET POTATO, PEELED AND SLICED

SALT AND FRESHLY GROUND BLACK PEPPER

2 LARGE CARROTS, PEELED AND SLICED

½ CUP PLUS 6 TABLESPOONS UNSALTED BUTTER

½ POUND (8 OUNCES) PHYLLO PASTRY, THAWED

¼ CUP PECAN PIECES, TOASTED AND FINELY CHOPPED

COARSE SEA SALT

¾ CUP CRÈME FRAÎCHE *(page 149)*

PUT THE CRANBERRIES and golden raisins in a small bowl and cover with hot water; set aside to plump for 10 minutes, then drain.

PUT THE POTATOES in a medium saucepan, cover with hot water, and add a little salt. Cook over high heat until fork-tender. Meanwhile, put the carrots in a small saucepan, cover with hot water, and add a little salt. Cook over high heat until fork-tender. Drain the potatoes and carrots in a strainer and set aside.

PUT THE BUTTER in a small saucepan over high heat. Let the butter melt and then stir continuously until the butter starts browning on the bottom of the pan. It will

also start bubbling and foaming a little. The butter should have a medium golden-brown color. Immediately pour the butter into a small dish and set aside.

SMASH THE SOFT-COOKED potatoes and carrots with a fork or handheld potato masher. You are looking for a lumpy consistency. Stir 6 tablespoons of the brown butter into the vegetables. Blend in the dried fruit and season to taste with salt and pepper.

PREHEAT THE OVEN to 375°F and fit a baking sheet with parchment paper or a nonstick baking mat. Unroll the phyllo dough and lay it flat on a clean work surface. The dimensions of the dough will be 9 by 13 inches, or

CONTINUED ➤

cut large sheets of phyllo dough to 9 by 13 inches. To help prevent the dough from drying out while working with it, cover with a slightly dampened clean kitchen cloth. Carefully place one sheet of dough on the prepared baking sheet. Brush with the melted brown butter, and lightly sprinkle with pecans and coarse sea salt. Lay another sheet on top and continue layering with brown butter, sea salt, and pecans. Layer and stack seven sheets together. Carefully spoon the vegetable-dried fruit filling along one of the long edges of the dough, packing it with your hands into a tubelike shape. Starting with the filling side of the dough, roll the strudel tightly into a log. Place the strudel in the center of the baking sheet, brush with the remaining butter, and sprinkle with pecans and a little sea salt.

PLACE IN THE CENTER of the oven and bake until golden brown, about 25 minutes. Remove the baking pan from the oven to a cooling rack. Transfer the strudel to a cutting board. With a serrated knife, cut the strudel using long sawing motions. This will help prevent excessive flaking of the pastry. Serve warm or at room temperature with spiced Crème Fraîche (see *Note*).

NOTE

Spice up homemade Crème Fraîche with a hint of ground cinnamon, nutmeg, allspice, and vanilla extract. Add as much or as little as your taste buds desire.

SEAFOOD STRUDEL

MAKES

4

SERVINGS

Tailor the herbs in the filling to what you feel like eating. I love tarragon, dill, and lemon with my fish, but adding roasted red peppers or sun-dried tomatoes can make a nice addition to the seafood filling. Serve for brunch with a side of Arugula Salad with Feta-Corn Vinaigrette (page 154).

1 CUP COOKED WHITE RICE

¼ CUP FROZEN PEAS, THAWED

¼ TEASPOON CHOPPED FRESH TARRAGON

½ TEASPOON SALT

1 TABLESPOON CHOPPED FRESH DILL

ZEST OF ½ LEMON

⅛ TEASPOON FRESHLY GROUND BLACK PEPPER

½ POUND (8 OUNCES) PHYLLO PASTRY, THAWED *(see page 15)*

4 TABLESPOONS UNSALTED BUTTER, MELTED

2 TABLESPOONS DRY BREAD CRUMBS

8 OUNCES RAW SHRIMP (70 TO 100), PEELED AND DEVEINED

8 OUNCES WILD SALMON FILLET, SKINNED AND CUT INTO 1-INCH PIECES

⅓ CUP CRUMBLED FETA CHEESE

PREHEAT THE OVEN to 400°F. Line a baking sheet with parchment paper or a nonstick baking mat. Combine the rice, peas, tarragon, and ¼ teaspoon of the salt in a small bowl. Combine the dill, lemon zest, the remaining ¼ teaspoon salt, and the pepper in another small bowl.

UNROLL THE PHYLLO DOUGH and lay it on a clean work surface. You should have a 9-by-13-inch rectangle. If the sheets are larger, trim to the desired size. To help prevent the dough from drying out while working with it, put a slightly dampened clean kitchen cloth over the top. Place one sheet of phyllo carefully on the prepared baking sheet and brush with melted butter. Overlap another phyllo sheet to form a 13-by-13-inch square.

Sprinkle lightly with bread crumbs. Continue, layering twelve total phyllo sheets with butter and bread crumbs in the same way, overlapping in the 13-by-13-inch square.

CAREFULLY SPOON the rice mixture along the length of one side of the dough, packing it with your hands into a tubelike shape. Top with the shrimp and salmon. Sprinkle with the dill mixture and the feta cheese. Starting with the filling side of the dough, roll the strudel tightly into a log. Brush with the remaining butter and dust with bread crumbs.

CENTER THE BAKING SHEET in the oven and bake until the crust is deep golden brown, about 30 minutes. Cut into 4 equal portions and serve warm.

FINGERLING POTATO AND CRISPY BACON PIZZAS

MAKES

6

I've been making these crispy breakfast, brunch, lunch, and appetizer pizzas for several years in my baking classes. Try my topping selections and then make your own signature pizzas using your favorite ingredients. Garnish each pizza wedge with a small dollop of Crème Fraîche (page 149), if desired, just before serving.

8 OUNCES FINGERLING POTATOES (*see* Note)

SALT

3 TEASPOONS FINELY CHOPPED FRESH THYME

2 TABLESPOONS MINCED RED ONION

6 SLICES SMOKED BACON, COOKED CRISP, DRAINED, AND CHOPPED

¼ CUP FINELY GRATED ASIAGO CHEESE (*see page 24*)

¼ CUP FINELY GRATED PARMESAN CHEESE (*see page 24*)

½ POUND (8 OUNCES) PHYLLO DOUGH, THAWED

½ CUP (1 STICK) UNSALTED BUTTER, MELTED

FRESHLY GROUND BLACK PEPPER

PUT THE POTATOES in a small saucepan, cover with water and add a little salt. Bring to a boil and cook until fork-tender. Drain, cool, and cut into ¼-inch-thick slices. Set aside. Put the thyme, onions, bacon, and cheeses in separate small bowls and set aside.

UNWRAP AND UNROLL the thawed phyllo dough, placing the stack on a work surface. Put a 6-inch plate on top of the phyllo and cut around the plate and through the stack of dough with a small sharp paring knife. Continue cutting until all the dough is cut into circles. Discard the scrap dough and stack all the circles together. Lay a lightly dampened clean kitchen cloth over the top to keep the dough moist.

PREHEAT THE OVEN to 400°F and line two baking sheets with parchment paper or nonstick baking mats. Place three phyllo circles on each prepared baking sheet.

Lightly brush all six circles with melted butter. Place another circle of dough on top of each of the first circles and brush again with melted butter. Continue until all six pizza circles are stacked with six layers of phyllo and butter. Put three to four slices of potato on top of each pizza stack. Sprinkle thyme, onions, and bacon over the potato slices, and top lightly with the two cheeses. Season to taste with pepper. Bake until medium golden brown, making sure the centers and bottoms of each crust are also golden brown, 12 to 15 minutes. Transfer to a cutting board and cut each pizza into 4 wedges using a sharp chef's knife or pizza wheel. Serve immediately.

NOTE

Fingerling potatoes are one of the many varieties of new potatoes that have a creamy, moist texture. When buying fingerling potatoes, look for their small and distinct fingerlike shape. If you have a difficult time finding them, substitute another low-starch potato like Yukon gold or red new potatoes. The potatoes and bacon can be cooked ahead and stored in the refrigerator for up to 1 day.

ROASTED RED PEPPER AND CRÈME FRAÎCHE QUICHE

Crème fraîche adds a delicate smoothness to the creamy custard in this quiche. I love the sweet roasted peppers and sometimes add roasted yellow and green peppers for additional color. Serve for lunch or brunch.

PASTRY DOUGH

1 ¾ CUPS ALL-PURPOSE FLOUR

¾ TEASPOON SALT

½ CUP (1 STICK) UNSALTED BUTTER, COLD AND CUT INTO CUBES

⅓ TO ⅔ CUP COLD WATER

FILLING

½ CUP WHOLE MILK

¾ CUP CRÈME FRAÎCHE *(page 149)*

1 CUP HEAVY (WHIPPING) CREAM

4 EGGS

2 EGG YOLKS

1 TEASPOON SALT

½ TEASPOON FRESHLY GROUND BLACK PEPPER

1 SMALL RED BELL PEPPER, ROASTED AND PEELED *(see page 25)*

TO PREPARE THE DOUGH, put the flour, salt, and butter in the bowl of a food processor fitted with a blade attachment. Pulse the mixture until the butter is pea size. Drizzle the water into the flour and pulse until the dough starts to form a ball. Turn the dough out onto a floured surface and knead once or twice. Pat into a flat disc about 1 inch thick. Wrap the dough in plastic film and chill for about 15 minutes before rolling.

MEANWHILE, PREPARE THE FILLING. Pour the milk and Crème Fraîche into a medium bowl and whisk until the mixture is smooth. Whisk in the heavy cream, eggs, egg yolks, salt, and pepper. Chop the roasted red peppers and stir them into the filling.

PREHEAT THE OVEN to 400°F and position a rack in the lower third of the oven. Put a 9-inch pie pan on a

baking sheet. Place the dough on a floured surface and dust the top with additional flour. Roll into a 12-inch circle about ¼ inch thick. Move the dough frequently to prevent it from sticking to the surface. Gently fold the dough in half; pick it up and place and unfold it evenly over the pie pan. Pat the dough firmly into the angled sides of the pan. There should be no air bubbles between the dough and the pan. Using kitchen shears or a small knife, trim excess dough flush with the pan to create a neat appearance. Make a decorative pattern on the rim of the pan by gently pressing the dough down with a fork. Place the pie pan on a flat baking sheet and partially blind bake (see page 23).

REMOVE THE BAKING SHEET from the oven. Transfer the baking sheet to a cooling rack and remove the foil and pie weights used to blind bake. Reduce the oven temperature to 325°F. Stir the filling briefly to remix, then pour it evenly into the prepared shell. Carefully return the baking sheet to the oven and continue to bake for 35 to 45 minutes. For a velvety custard, be sure to cook the filling to a soft-set consistency. To check for doneness, gently shake the quiche. The center will be slightly soft and jiggling. Additionally, a thin knife can be inserted into the center of the custard; if it comes out clean, the custard is set and can be removed from the oven.

PLACE THE QUICHE on the cooling rack and let cool for 10 minutes. Cut into wedges with a sharp knife and serve warm or at room temperature. Cover any leftover quiche with plastic film and refrigerate for up to 3 days. Warm the quiche in a 325°F oven for about 15 minutes before serving.

CHÈVRE QUICHE WITH
RED AND GREEN GRAPES

Warm, juicy grapes, which burst in your mouth, are a nice addition to the tangy goat cheese custard in this quiche. Make it the star of your next brunch. Add a dusting of fresh thyme just before serving.

PASTRY DOUGH

1¾ CUPS ALL-PURPOSE FLOUR

2 TEASPOONS CHOPPED FRESH THYME, OR
1 TEASPOON DRIED

¾ TEASPOON SALT

½ CUP (1 STICK) COLD UNSALTED BUTTER, CUT INTO
½-INCH CUBES

⅓ TO ⅔ CUP COLD WATER

FILLING

4 OUNCES CHÈVRE (*see* Note)

½ CUP HALF-AND-HALF

4 EGGS

2 EGG YOLKS

1 CUP HEAVY (WHIPPING) CREAM

½ TEASPOON SALT

½ CUP SEEDLESS RED GRAPES

½ CUP SEEDLESS GREEN GRAPES

TO PREPARE THE DOUGH, put the flour, thyme, salt, and butter in the bowl of a food processor fitted with a blade attachment. Pulse the mixture until the butter is pea-size. Drizzle the water into the flour and pulse until the dough starts to form a ball. Turn the dough out on a floured surface and knead once or twice. Wrap the dough in plastic film, pressing into a flat disc about 1 inch thick, and chill about for 15 minutes before rolling.

MEANWHILE, PREPARE THE FILLING. Break up the cheese and put it in the bowl of a food processor fitted with a blade attachment. Add the half-and-half and blend until smooth, about 15 seconds. Add the eggs, egg yolks, cream, and salt. Blend for another 15 seconds, then pour into a container with a spout.

PREHEAT THE OVEN to 400°F and position a rack in the lower third of the oven. Put a 9-inch pie pan on a

baking sheet. Place the dough on a floured surface and dust the top with additional flour. Roll into a 12-inch circle about ¼ inch thick. Move the dough frequently to prevent it from sticking to the surface. Gently fold the dough in half; pick it up and place and unfold it evenly over the pie pan. Pat the dough firmly into the angled sides of the pan. There should be no air bubbles between the dough and the pan. Using kitchen shears or a small knife, trim excess dough flush with the pan to make a neat appearance. Make a decorative pattern on the rim by pressing down with a fork. Place the pie pan on a flat baking sheet and blind bake (see page 23).

REMOVE THE BAKING SHEET from the oven. Transfer the baking sheet to a cooling rack and remove the foil and pie weights used to blind bake. Reduce the oven temperature to 325°F. Add the grapes to the custard, then pour it evenly into the prepared shell. Carefully return the baking sheet to the oven and continue to bake for 35 to 45 minutes. To check for doneness, gently shake the quiche. The center will be slightly soft and jiggling. Additionally, the tip of a thin knife can be inserted in the center of the custard; if it comes out clean, the quiche is done.

PLACE THE BAKED QUICHE on the cooling rack and cool for 10 minutes. Cut into wedges with a sharp knife and serve warm or at room temperature. Cover any leftover quiche with plastic film and refrigerate for up to 3 days. Warm the quiche by placing it in a preheated 325°F oven for about 15 minutes.

NOTE

Chèvre means "goat" in French. It is a delightfully tangy cheese. To ensure the cheese is made of pure goat's milk, look for "pur chèvre" on the label; cheeses not labeled thusly may have had cows' milk added. The texture can range from moist and creamy to dry and semifirm. Chèvre can be stored, tightly wrapped, in the refrigerator for up to 2 weeks.

SPINACH AND FETA
DOUBLE-CRUST PIE

The buttery crust, zesty feta cheese, and toasted pine nuts add layers of flavor and texture to make this pie a lunch or brunch star! Dried currants bring a touch of sweetness to every bite.

PASTRY DOUGH

3½ CUPS ALL-PURPOSE FLOUR

1½ TEASPOONS SALT

1¼ CUPS UNSALTED BUTTER, COLD AND CUT INTO ½-INCH CUBES

¾ TO 1 CUP ICE WATER

SPINACH-LEEK FILLING

2 TABLESPOONS EXTRA-VIRGIN OLIVE OIL

2 LARGE LEEKS, WHITE PARTS ONLY, WASHED AND THINLY SLICED

1 TEASPOON SALT

24 OUNCES FROZEN CHOPPED SPINACH, THAWED AND SQUEEZED OF WATER

½ CUP PINE NUTS, TOASTED

½ CUP DRIED CURRANTS

½ TEASPOON FRESHLY GRATED NUTMEG

1 TEASPOON GRATED LEMON ZEST

1½ TEASPOONS FRESH LEMON JUICE

½ CUP HEAVY (WHIPPING) CREAM

3 EGGS

6 OUNCES (¾ CUP) FETA CHEESE, CRUMBLED

SESAME SEEDS FOR GARNISH (*optional*)

TO PREPARE THE PASTRY DOUGH, put the flour, salt, and butter in the bowl of a food processor fitted with a blade attachment. Pulse until the butter is pea-size. Drizzle the water and pulse until the dough starts to form a ball. Remove the dough and flatten into two 1-inch-thick discs. Wrap in plastic film and refrigerate.

TO PREPARE THE FILLING, heat the oil in a large sauté pan or skillet. Add the leeks and salt. Cook until tender, 3 to 4 minutes. Put the leeks into a large bowl and add the spinach, pine nuts, currants, nutmeg, lemon zest and lemon juice, the cream, and 2 of the eggs. Stir well to combine.

PREHEAT THE OVEN to 375°F and position a rack in the lower third of the oven. Put a 9-inch pie pan on a baking sheet. Place one disc of dough on a floured surface and dust the top with additional flour. Roll into a 12-inch circle about ¼ inch thick. Move the dough frequently to prevent it from sticking to the surface. Gently fold the dough in half; pick it up and place and unfold it evenly over the pie pan. Pat the dough firmly into the angled sides of the pan. There should be no air bubbles between the dough and the pan. Leave the excess dough hanging over the edge of the pie pan. Pour the filling into the dough-lined pan and sprinkle with feta cheese.

BRUSH A LITTLE OF THE REMAINING EGG on the rim of the dough that is already in the pan. Roll the remaining dough into a 12-inch circle and center it on top of the filling. Gently press the top and bottom pastries together around the rim with your fingertips. Trim the excess dough to the rim of the pan. Make a decorative pattern around the rim by gently pressing the dough down with a fork. Break the remaining egg into a small bowl and lightly beat it. Brush the entire top of the pie with a little of the beaten egg and make a small slit in the center of the pie with a sharp knife so steam can escape while the pie is baking. Bake on the lower rack of the oven for 40 minutes. Remove from the oven, brush the pie with more of the beaten egg, and sprinkle with sesame seeds, if using. Return the pie to the oven and bake until deep golden brown, another 10 minutes. Remove to a baking rack, cut into wedges, and serve warm. Leftover pie can be wrapped and refrigerated for up to 3 days. Warm for 10 to 15 minutes in a 325°F oven.

DEEP-DISH CURRIED VEGETABLE POTPIES WITH DRIED FRUITS

Earthy vegetables, sweet figs, and currants are all flavored with fragrant spices to make a warm vegetarian curry meal. Golden flaky pastry crowns each individual crock for a satisfying meal, or make one large casserole and spoon out smaller portions to serve as a side dish. For curry lovers, increase the spices to your liking.

PASTRY DOUGH

1¾ CUPS ALL-PURPOSE FLOUR

¾ TEASPOON SALT

½ CUP (1 STICK) UNSALTED BUTTER, COLD AND CUT INTO ½-INCH CUBES

⅓ CUP COLD WATER

VEGETABLE FILLING

2½ TABLESPOONS CANOLA OR VEGETABLE OIL

½ LARGE RED ONION, PEELED AND CUT INTO ½-INCH DICE

2 CARROTS, PEELED AND SLICED

1 SMALL RED BELL PEPPER, TRIMMED AND SEEDED, CUT INTO ½-INCH DICE

1½ TEASPOONS SALT PLUS MORE TO TASTE

2 GARLIC CLOVES, SLICED

1 TABLESPOON CURRY POWDER

½ TEASPOON DRIED GROUND GINGER

¼ TEASPOON FRESHLY GROUND BLACK PEPPER, PLUS MORE TO TASTE

¼ TEASPOON GROUND CINNAMON

⅛ TEASPOON GROUND ALLSPICE

3 CUPS WATER

2 CUPS CAULIFLOWER FLORETS (1 SMALL CAULIFLOWER)

2 CUPS PEELED AND CHOPPED YAMS (1 LARGE YAM)

⅓ CUP CURRANTS

12 DRIED FIGS, STEMMED AND HALVED

2 TEASPOONS CORNSTARCH

1 TABLESPOON FRESH LEMON JUICE

1 EGG, SLIGHTLY BEATEN

CONTINUED ➤

TO PREPARE THE DOUGH, put the flour, salt, and butter in the bowl of a food processor fitted with a blade attachment. Pulse the mixture until the butter is pea-size, about 10 seconds. Drizzle the water into the flour and pulse until the dough starts to come together. Put the dough on a lightly floured work surface and knead once or twice. Wrap the dough in plastic film, pat into a 1-inch-thick disc, and refrigerate for 30 minutes before using (see *Note*).

MEANWHILE, PREPARE THE FILLING. Heat the oil in a large pot over medium heat. Add the onions, carrots, and red peppers. Stir to coat them in the oil. Add the 1½ teaspoons salt and sauté the vegetables for 3 minutes. Add the garlic, curry powder, ginger, ¼ teaspoon pepper, the cinnamon, and allspice and sauté for 1 minute. Stir in the water, cauliflower, yams, currants, and figs. Bring the mixture to a simmer. Partially cover the pot with a lid, and simmer until the yams are tender, about 20 minutes (see *Note*).

PUT THE CORNSTARCH in a small bowl and stir in 2 tablespoons of the simmering vegetable liquid to make a smooth paste. Pour the cornstarch into the hot vegetables and gently stir to combine. Simmer for 3 minutes to thicken the liquid, then add the lemon juice. Season to taste with salt and pepper. Remove the pot from the heat and divide heaping cups of the curried vegetables among six 12-ounce (1½-cup) ceramic baking dishes or ceramic crocks.

PREHEAT THE OVEN to 400°F. Place the dough on a floured surface and dust the top with additional flour. Roll into a large disc about $^1/_8$ inch thick. Cut out six circles slightly larger than the top of each baking dish. Place a pastry disc over the top of each vegetable dish and push down gently to adhere the dough to the edges of each dish. Lightly brush the pastry with a little beaten egg and puncture the tops in three spots with a sharp paring knife to allow the steam to escape. Place the baking dishes on a baking sheet. Place into the oven and bake until the crust is deep golden brown, 20 to 25 minutes. Serve hot from the oven.

NOTE

Wrap freshly made dough airtight in plastic film and refrigerate for up to 2 days or freeze for up to 1 month. Thaw frozen pastry in the refrigerator overnight, and then roll the dough as directed. The filling can be made 2 days ahead and gently reheated just before pouring into the ceramic dishes.

GRILLED-VEGETABLE GALETTE

MAKES

8

SERVINGS

Grilled vegetables peek out from the top of this attractive tart. The flaky pastry made with cream cheese and oregano highlights summer's freshest vegetables. Use the vegetables suggested or use your own favorites. Serve warm as a first course, for a light lunch, or as a side dish with meat or fish entrées.

GALETTE DOUGH

1 CUP (2 STICKS) UNSALTED BUTTER AT ROOM TEMPERATURE

ONE 8-OUNCE PACKAGE CREAM CHEESE AT ROOM TEMPERATURE

2 CUPS ALL-PURPOSE FLOUR

2 TEASPOONS DRIED OREGANO

FILLING

1 MEDIUM PORTOBELLO MUSHROOM, STEMMED AND SLICED

1 MEDIUM ZUCCHINI, CUT INTO ½-INCH ROUNDS

1 MEDIUM YELLOW SQUASH, CUT INTO LONG STRIPS, ¼-INCH THICK

1 JAPANESE EGGPLANT, CUT INTO LONG STRIPS, ¼-INCH THICK

½ MEDIUM RED BELL PEPPER, ROASTED AND PEELED *(see page 25)*

1 RED ONION, PEELED AND CUT INTO 1-INCH SLICES

½ CUP EXTRA-VIRGIN OLIVE OIL

SALT AND FRESHLY GROUND BLACK PEPPER

1 EGG, LIGHTLY BEATEN

TO PREPARE THE DOUGH, put the butter and cream cheese in the bowl of a food processor fitted with a blade attachment. Process for 1 minute, then scrape the sides of the bowl with a rubber spatula. Add the flour and oregano and pulse until the mixture starts to form into a ball. Remove the dough from the bowl and knead once or twice. Pat into a 1-inch-thick disc. Wrap in plastic film and refrigerate until firm, about 30 minutes.

MEANWHILE, PREPARE THE FILLING. Preheat a grill and brush the prepared vegetables with olive oil and season to taste with salt and pepper. Grill on both sides until slightly tender and browned. Put the vegetables in a bowl after grilling and toss with a little more olive oil and additional salt and pepper, if desired.

PREHEAT THE OVEN to 400°F and line a baking sheet with parchment paper or a nonstick baking mat. Place the dough on a floured work surface, and dust the top with additional flour. Roll into a 12-inch circle. Pile the grilled vegetables in the center of the rolled pastry and spread out to within 2 inches of the edge. Pull the dough up and over the vegetables, pleating the dough and leaving an opening to create a partially open-faced tart. The final size of the galette will be about 10 inches in diameter. Brush a little beaten egg on the crust. Center on the prepared baking sheet and bake in the oven until the crust is deep golden brown, about 35 minutes. Remove the baking sheet from the oven and transfer to a cooling rack. Cut the galette into wedges and

COBBLERS

CRUMBLES

BETTIES

BREAD
PUDDINGS

SHORT
CAKES

DUMPLINGS

CHEESE
CAKES

RUSTIC

Ahhh, the feeling of well-being and contentment! Home-style cooking, snuggling up with a blanket by the fireplace, and favorite family recipes all make me dream of heaping spoonfuls of bubbling-hot casseroles right out of the oven. Thoughts of yummy Chicken Dijon Brown Betty with crusty bread or Creamy Sweet Corn and Prosciutto Crisp alongside a honey-baked ham make my mouth water. These creative rustic dishes utilize some of the simple quick bread techniques and encourage you to enjoy the comfort of baking.

SPICY TOMATO CRUMBLE

MAKES

4–6

SERVINGS

This delicious puttanesca-style dish with a crunchy topping is great with grilled fish. For an interesting change, scoop a large spoonful on top of fresh-cooked pasta.

TOPPING

⅓ CUP DRY BREAD CRUMBS

¼ CUP ROLLED OATS

I TABLESPOON ALL-PURPOSE FLOUR

¼ CUP FINELY GRATED PARMESAN CHEESE
(see page 24)

I TEASPOON DRIED OREGANO

½ TEASPOON DRIED SAGE

¼ TEASPOON SALT

2 TABLESPOONS UNSALTED BUTTER, COLD AND CUT
INTO CUBES

FILLING

3 GARLIC CLOVES, MINCED

I TABLESPOON CAPERS, RINSED, DRAINED, AND
ROUGHLY CHOPPED

2 TABLESPOONS FINELY DICED PEPPERONCINI
(see Note*)*

2 TEASPOONS CLOVER HONEY

I TEASPOON DRIED BASIL

½ CUP DRY RED WINE

ONE 28-OUNCE CAN WHOLE ITALIAN TOMATOES
WITH JUICE, ROUGHLY CHOPPED

½ CUP KALAMATA OLIVES, ROUGHLY CHOPPED

TO PREPARE THE TOPPING, combine the bread crumbs, rolled oats, flour, Parmesan cheese, oregano, sage, and salt in a medium bowl. Add the butter and work it into the flour mixture with your fingertips until the mixture is crumbly. Set aside.

TO PREPARE THE FILLING, put the garlic, capers, pepperoncini, honey, basil, red wine, tomatoes, and olives in a medium saucepan over high heat. Stir and bring to a rapid boil. Reduce the heat to medium and cook for 25 minutes to reduce the filling slightly.

PREHEAT THE OVEN to 350°F. Pour the filling into one 6-cup (1½-quart) casserole dish and sprinkle with the topping. Place the casserole dish on a baking sheet and center in the oven. Bake until the topping is golden brown and the filling is bubbling, about 15 minutes. Serve hot from the oven.

NOTE

Pepperoncini are also known as "Tuscan peppers." They are medium-hot in taste with a slightly sweet flavor. A few of these chopped peppers will add an uplifting kick to a sandwich, or they can be stirred into tomato dishes to add pizzazz. They come pickled and are available in most supermarkets.

CREAMY SWEET CORN AND PROSCIUTTO CRISP

MAKES
6
SERVINGS

Try this crunchy dish with the season's best corn, which is usually at its peak after the Fourth of July. When fresh corn isn't available or to save a little time, use canned or frozen yellow or white corn.

TOPPING

¼ CUP ALL-PURPOSE FLOUR

¼ CUP ROLLED OATS

½ CUP JAPANESE BREAD CRUMBS (PANKO)

⅛ TEASPOON SALT

2 TEASPOONS FINELY CHOPPED FRESH SAGE

3 TABLESPOONS UNSALTED BUTTER AT ROOM TEMPERATURE

1 EGG YOLK

FILLING

2 TABLESPOONS UNSALTED BUTTER

¼ CUP FINELY CHOPPED SHALLOTS

¼ CUP FINELY CHOPPED RED BELL PEPPER

¼ CUP FINELY CHOPPED CELERY

2½ CUPS FRESH CORN KERNELS, 3 TO 4 EARS (*see* Note)

3 THIN SLICES OF PROSCIUTTO, TORN INTO 1-INCH PIECES

SALT AND FRESHLY GROUND BLACK PEPPER

2 TEASPOONS FINELY CHOPPED FRESH SAGE

¾ CUP HALF-AND-HALF

¾ CUP WHOLE MILK

TO PREPARE THE TOPPING, combine the flour, rolled oats, bread crumbs, salt, and sage in a medium bowl. Add the butter and work it into the dry ingredients with your fingers until the mixture looks like a coarse, crumbly meal. Add the egg yolk and lightly mix. The topping will be slightly sticky, but crumbly. Set aside.

TO PREPARE THE FILLING, melt the butter in a large skillet over high heat. Add the shallots, red pepper, celery, corn, and prosciutto. Season to taste with salt and pepper and sauté for 5 minutes, stirring occasionally. Stir in the sage, half-and-half, and milk. Bring to a rapid boil and continue cooking for 2 minutes, then remove the pan from the heat.

PREHEAT THE OVEN to 350°F and place six 6-ounce (¾-cup) ceramic baking dishes on a baking sheet. Spoon equal amounts of the hot corn mixture into each dish. Divide the topping evenly over each portion. Place the baking sheet in the oven and bake until the corn filling is bubbling and the top is golden brown, 10 to 15 minutes. Serve warm as a side dish with your favorite meat, fish, or poultry entrée.

NOTE

For shucking and cutting fresh corn kernels, pull the husks off each ear and then remove the silk. Stand an ear on its stem end on top of a cutting board or in a wide bowl. Using a sharp knife, cut off the kernels, from top to bottom, three to four rows at a time.

MUSTARD-RUBBED MINI LAMB SANDWICHES ON MINT SHORTCAKES

Freshly ground lamb has the best flavor; ask your butcher to grind some if you don't see it already freshly ground. The mint-scented shortcake-style buns are delicious with the juicy mini burgers. A small sandwich makes a quick, tasty lunch or snack.

MARINADE

2 TABLESPOONS DIJON MUSTARD

2 TABLESPOONS WATER

1 TEASPOON SOY SAUCE

2 TEASPOONS MINCED FRESH ROSEMARY

2 TEASPOONS CLOVER HONEY

1 POUND FRESHLY GROUND LAMB

SALT AND FRESHLY GROUND BLACK PEPPER

MINT SHORTCAKES

1 CUP ALL-PURPOSE FLOUR

1 TEASPOON BAKING POWDER

1 TABLESPOON FINELY CHOPPED FRESH MINT

¾ TEASPOON SALT

1 TEASPOON GRANULATED SUGAR

¼ CUP (½ STICK) UNSALTED BUTTER, COLD AND CUT INTO ½-INCH CUBES

½ CUP WHOLE MILK

APRICOT-MINT RELISH *(page 151; optional)*

TO PREPARE THE MARINADE, stir the mustard, water, soy sauce, rosemary, and honey together in a small bowl.

PUT THE GROUND LAMB into a medium bowl and season to taste with salt and pepper. Form the meat into six small patties. Put the patties on a plate and pour the marinade over them; cover and refrigerate for 30 minutes, or until ready to grill.

TO PREPARE THE SHORTCAKES, preheat the oven to 375°F and line the bottom of a baking sheet with parchment paper or a nonstick baking mat. Put the flour, baking powder, mint, salt, and sugar in the bowl of a food processor fitted with a blade attachment. Add the butter and pulse until the mixture resembles coarse meal, about 10 seconds. Pour in the milk and pulse until the mixture starts to form into a dough. This will only take a few seconds. Don't overprocess and don't worry if you see a few dry flour patches.

SPOON THE DOUGH onto the prepared baking sheet in six equal mounds and put the baking sheet in the oven. Bake until the shortcakes are lightly browned and spring back when gently touched in the center, 10 to 12 minutes. Place on a cooling rack while cooking the lamb.

PREHEAT A GRILL or set the oven on broil. Cook the lamb patties on both sides until the desired doneness is reached. Carefully split each shortcake bun with a serrated knife and top with a lamb patty. If desired, serve the sandwiches with Apricot-Mint Relish.

ONION, FENNEL, AND ORANGE UPSIDE-DOWN SHORTCAKE

Sherry, balsamic vinegar, and fennel give a crowning touch to the fresh, orange-scented shortcake. For a satisfying meal, enjoy a slice with roasted pork tenderloin.

ONION FILLING

3 TABLESPOONS EXTRA-VIRGIN OLIVE OIL

3 MEDIUM ONIONS, THINLY SLICED

½ CUP DRY SHERRY

2 TABLESPOONS BROWN SUGAR

½ CUP BALSAMIC VINEGAR

1 TABLESPOON FENNEL SEEDS, TOASTED AND CRUSHED

1½ TEASPOONS SALT

¼ TEASPOON FRESHLY GROUND BLACK PEPPER

½ CUP WATER

1 SMALL RED BELL PEPPER, ROASTED, PEELED, AND ROUGHLY CHOPPED *(see page 25)*

SHORTCAKE

2 CUPS ALL-PURPOSE FLOUR

1 TABLESPOON BAKING POWDER

1 TEASPOON SALT

ZEST OF 1 MEDIUM ORANGE

6 TABLESPOONS UNSALTED BUTTER, COLD AND CUT INTO ½-INCH CUBES

1 CUP WHOLE MILK

TO PREPARE THE ONION FILLING, put the olive oil, onions, sherry, brown sugar, vinegar, fennel seeds, salt, and pepper in a large sauté pan or wide-bottomed skillet over medium-high heat. Cover and cook for 25 minutes, stirring occasionally to prevent the onions from sticking. Stir in the water. Add the roasted red peppers to the onions. Cover, reduce the heat to medium, and cook for an additional 15 minutes, stirring often. Remove from the heat. Cut a piece of aluminum foil to fit the bottom of a 9-inch round cake pan. Place it in the bottom of the pan and generously oil or spray the foil and the sides of the pan. Spread the onions evenly in the pan, reserving some to spoon over the finished cake.

TO PREPARE THE SHORTCAKE, preheat the oven to 350°F. Put the flour, baking powder, salt, and orange zest in the bowl of a food processor fitted with a blade attachment. Add the butter and pulse for 10 seconds or until the butter is pea-size. Add the milk and pulse until the mixture starts to form into a dough. Carefully spread the dough over the onions, leaving no gaps and making sure the edges of the pan are covered with dough. Put the pan in the oven and bake just until the top of the cake feels firm in the center when lightly pressed, about 30 minutes (the top will not look brown). Transfer to a rack and let cool for 5 minutes.

RUN A SHARP KNIFE around the inside of the pan. Place and hold a large serving plate over the top of the pan and invert the cake onto the plate. Carefully remove the cake pan and foil. Spoon the reserved onions over the cake. Cut into wedges and serve warm.

CANADIAN BACON BREAD PUDDING

Meaty Canadian bacon, delicately flavored custard cream, and tender biscuit-type bread—a comfort meal that works well served with a fresh fruit salad for breakfast, brunch, or a light supper. Enjoy the featured bread or substitute Chile-Cheese Bread with a spicy kick (see Note).

BREAD

1¼ CUPS ALL-PURPOSE FLOUR

1½ TEASPOONS BAKING POWDER

½ TEASPOON BAKING SODA

½ TEASPOON SALT

1 TEASPOON GRANULATED SUGAR

½ CUP PLUS 2 TABLESPOONS SOUR CREAM

½ CUP HEAVY (WHIPPING) CREAM

CUSTARD FILLING

3 EGGS

3 EGG YOLKS

2 TABLESPOONS WHOLE-GRAIN MUSTARD

3 CUPS HEAVY (WHIPPING) CREAM

1 TEASPOON SALT

½ TEASPOON FRESHLY GROUND PEPPER

12 OUNCES CANADIAN BACON, RIND REMOVED, CUT INTO ¼-INCH CUBES OR ½-INCH STRIPS

NOTE

Chile-Cheese Bread (page 51) is an excellent bread alternative. It can be torn into about 1-inch chunks and put into the casserole dish. Add the Canadian bacon and pour the custard (omitting the mustard) over the top. Bake as directed.

TO PREPARE THE BREAD, preheat the oven to 350°F and butter or spray the bottom of an 8-inch baking pan. Stir the flour, baking powder, baking soda, salt, and sugar together in a large bowl, gently blending the ingredients. Whisk the sour cream and heavy cream together in a small bowl until smooth. Pour the cream mixture over the flour mixture and mix gently with a rubber spatula. Spoon the soft dough into the prepared baking pan and spread just a little; don't worry about all the dough touching the sides of the pan completely. Bake until the top springs back when gently touched in the center and the crust is pale in color, about 20 minutes. Remove from the oven and place on a cooling rack.

MEANWHILE, PREPARE THE FILLING. Butter or spray a 9-by-13-inch casserole dish. Whisk the eggs, egg yolks, and mustard together in a medium bowl. Stir the cream, salt, and pepper into the eggs. Set aside.

TEAR THE BREAD into large 1-inch chunks and spread the chunks evenly into the prepared casserole dish. Sprinkle the Canadian bacon over the top of the bread, then carefully pour the custard evenly over the top. Cover the casserole with aluminum foil and set it inside a slightly larger pan. Place the doubled pan in the oven and pour hot water into the outer pan until it reaches about one-third of the way up the sides of the casserole. Take care not to splash water into the bread pudding. Bake until the custard is set but the center still jiggles slightly when you shake the pan, about 1 hour. Carefully remove the pans from the oven; lift out the casserole from the water bath and set it on a cooling rack. Discard the water bath when the water has reached room temperature. Serve the bread pudding warm. Cover and refrigerate any leftovers for up to 3 days. Heat foil-covered leftover bread pudding in a 350°F oven for about 15 minutes

CHICKEN DIJON BROWN BETTY

I enjoy this appetite-pleasing comfort meal any time of year. Chicken and fennel—a wonderful combination with a touch of hearty mustard, honey, and cream—is topped with crunchy browned crumbs. Try it hot from the oven with roasted corn on the cob, crusty sourdough rolls, and a crisp salad.

TOPPING

⅓ CUP DRY BREAD CRUMBS

½ CUP JAPANESE BREAD CRUMBS (PANKO)

½ TEASPOON SALT

¼ TEASPOON FRESHLY GROUND BLACK PEPPER

2 TABLESPOONS UNSALTED BUTTER, MELTED

2 TABLESPOONS FINELY CHOPPED FRESH PARSLEY

CHICKEN DIJON FILLING

1 TABLESPOON UNSALTED BUTTER

½ CUP CHOPPED YELLOW ONION

1 SMALL FENNEL BULB, QUARTERED, CORED, AND THINLY SLICED

½ TEASPOON SALT

1 POUND BONELESS AND SKINLESS CHICKEN THIGHS, CUT INTO 1-INCH PIECES

2 TABLESPOONS DRY WHITE WINE OR CHICKEN BROTH

1½ CUPS HEAVY (WHIPPING) CREAM

3 TABLESPOONS DIJON MUSTARD

1 TABLESPOON CLOVER HONEY

¼ TEASPOON FRESHLY GROUND WHITE PEPPER

TO PREPARE THE TOPPING, put the dry bread crumbs, Japanese bread crumbs, salt, and pepper in a small bowl. Stir in the melted butter and 1 tablespoon of the chopped parsley. Set aside (see Note).

TO PREPARE THE FILLING, preheat the oven to 375°F. Butter or spray four 8-ounce (1-cup) ceramic ramekins and arrange them on a baking sheet. Melt the butter in a large sauté pan or skillet over medium heat. Add the onions, fennel, and salt. Cook until soft and tender, 4 to 5 minutes, stirring occasionally.

ADD THE CHICKEN PIECES, nestling them down into the bottom of the pan. Continue to sauté until the chicken is cooked through, another 3 to 5 minutes. Add the white wine and stir to scrape up any caramelized bits on the bottom of the pan. Stir in the cream, Dijon mustard, honey, and pepper. Bring the mixture to a rapid boil and cook for 1 minute to reduce the sauce slightly. Divide the chicken mixture equally among the prepared ramekins, and sprinkle each with 3 tablespoons of the topping.

CENTER THE BAKING SHEET in the oven and bake until golden brown on top and bubbling around the edges, about 15 minutes. Remove from the oven and sprinkle each ramekin with the remaining chopped parsley. Serve piping hot from the oven.

NOTE

The topping and filling can be made up to 1 day in advance. For the filling, cook as directed, divide among the ramekins, wrap, and refrigerate. Make the prepared topping, pour it into a small bowl, wrap tightly, and store in the refrigerator. Preheat the oven to 375°F. Microwave the prepared filled ramekins on high for 30 seconds each. Place on a baking sheet, sprinkle with the topping, and bake, as directed.

YUKON GOLD BROWN BETTY

My savory betty combines light sherry wine and thyme vinaigrette tossed with thin slices of potato and fennel. The topping is simple and straightforward but adds a crunchy texture to the finished dish.

TOPPING

⅓ CUP DRY BREAD CRUMBS

1 TABLESPOON FINELY CHOPPED FRESH THYME

⅛ TEASPOON SALT

PINCH OF GARLIC POWDER

2 TABLESPOONS UNSALTED BUTTER, MELTED

FILLING

⅓ CUP EXTRA-VIRGIN OLIVE OIL

2 TABLESPOONS WATER

¼ CUP LIGHT SHERRY WINE VINEGAR

1 TEASPOON FRESH LEMON JUICE

1 TABLESPOON FINELY CHOPPED FRESH THYME

1 TEASPOON GRATED LEMON ZEST

2 TABLESPOONS MINCED SHALLOTS

3 GARLIC CLOVES, MINCED

1½ TEASPOONS SALT

1 TEASPOON FRESHLY GROUND BLACK PEPPER

1 POUND YUKON GOLD POTATOES, VERY THINLY SLICED *(see page 15)*

1 MEDIUM FENNEL BULB, VERY THINLY SLICED

TO PREPARE THE TOPPING, stir all the ingredients together in a small bowl and set aside.

TO PREPARE THE FILLING, preheat the oven to 375°F. Put all the ingredients into a large bowl and toss together. Spread the filling evenly into an 8-by-8-inch baking dish and cover with aluminum foil. Place on a baking sheet and put into the oven. Bake until the potatoes and fennel are fork-tender, about 1 hour. Remove the casserole from the oven. Remove the aluminum foil and sprinkle the topping evenly over the potatoes.

RETURN TO THE OVEN uncovered and bake until bubbly and the topping is golden brown, 15 to 20 minutes. Serve immediately as a side dish.

CONFETTI CORN BREAD-CRUSTED CREOLE SHRIMP

I love the taste of buttery corn bread and the texture of the filling and the topping. This is a great dish to eat with soup spoons. For an attractive presentation, spoon generous portions into pretty rimmed soup bowls or bake in individual casserole dishes or crocks. To save time, make the Creole Shrimp Filling a day ahead (see Note).

CREOLE SHRIMP FILLING

4 TABLESPOONS UNSALTED BUTTER

1 MEDIUM ONION, CHOPPED

2 STALKS CELERY, THINLY SLICED

½ GREEN BELL PEPPER, CHOPPED

2 GARLIC CLOVES, MINCED

1 TABLESPOON CREOLE SEASONING

2 TABLESPOONS FLOUR

ONE 14-OUNCE CAN DICED TOMATOES

½ CUP TOMATO SAUCE

1 CUP CHICKEN BROTH

1 BAY LEAF

8 OUNCES BAY SHRIMP

TOPPING

½ CUP (1 STICK) UNSALTED BUTTER AT ROOM TEMPERATURE

2 TEASPOONS GRANULATED SUGAR

2 EGGS AT ROOM TEMPERATURE

¼ CUP PEELED AND DICED MILD GREEN CHILES, FRESH OR CANNED (DRAINED)

½ CUP CORN KERNELS

½ CUP CANNED CREAM-STYLE CORN

2 TABLESPOONS FINELY CHOPPED RED BELL PEPPER

2 TABLESPOONS FINELY CHOPPED GREEN BELL PEPPER

½ CUP ALL-PURPOSE FLOUR

½ CUP YELLOW CORNMEAL

1 TABLESPOON BAKING POWDER

½ TEASPOON SALT

TO PREPARE THE FILLING, melt the butter in a large sauté pan or skillet over high heat. Add the onion, celery, and bell peppers. Cook until the vegetables are tender, about 3 minutes. Stir in the garlic and Creole seasoning, and cook until the garlic is fragrant, about 1 minute. Sprinkle the flour over the vegetables and stir constantly, about 2 minutes, until slightly thickened. Add the diced tomatoes, tomato sauce, chicken broth, and bay leaf. Stir and bring to a simmer. Reduce the heat to medium, cover the pan with a lid, and cook for 5 minutes. Add the shrimp and heat through, about 2 minutes. Remove the bay leaf and pour the filling into an 8-by-8-inch square or round baking dish. Set aside in a warm area, while preparing the topping.

CONTINUED ➤

TO PREPARE THE TOPPING, preheat the oven to 375°F. Put the butter and sugar in the bowl of a stand mixer fitted with a paddle attachment. Whip on medium speed until light and fluffy, about 2 minutes. Incorporate the eggs one at a time and mix until smooth. Add the green chiles, creamed corn, red and green bell peppers, the flour, cornmeal, baking powder, and salt. Mix on low speed until the mixture forms a soft batter.

CAREFULLY DOLLOP the corn bread topping over the filling. Using an offset metal spatula, spread the batter smoothly across the top of the casserole, forming a thin layer. Place the baking dish on a baking sheet in the center of the oven. Bake until the topping is golden brown and the filling is bubbling around the edges, about 40 minutes. Remove from the oven to a cooling rack. Cut through the corn bread with a small knife. Scoop 6 to 8 generous portions of the filling and the corn bread into large soup bowls or onto plates.

NOTE

To save time, I like to make the filling a day ahead. Put the cooked shrimp mixture in the casserole dish, wrap in aluminum foil, and refrigerate. When you're ready to serve, preheat the oven to 375°F. Put the covered casserole on a baking sheet and into the oven to warm, about 20 minutes. Meanwhile, make the corn-bread topping, spread it over the warm filling, and continue baking until bubbly and golden brown, 40 to 50 minutes.

STILTON CHEESECAKE ON A CANDIED-WALNUT CRUST

The bold flavor of Stilton mellows and blends well with rich sour cream and cream cheese. Bite into the sweet port-poached walnut crust while savoring the cake's smooth texture. Serve thin slices alongside crispy wafers and a salad of field greens tossed with fresh figs, when they're in season.

CANDIED WALNUTS

1 CUP RUBY PORT

2 TABLESPOONS GRANULATED SUGAR

¾ CUP WALNUT PIECES

CRUST

½ CUP CRUSHED WHOLE-WHEAT CRACKERS

¼ TEASPOON FRESHLY GROUND BLACK PEPPER

2 TABLESPOONS UNSALTED BUTTER, MELTED

1 TABLESPOON FIG JAM (*see* NOTE)

FILLING

TWO 8-OUNCE PACKAGES CREAM CHEESE AT ROOM TEMPERATURE

4 OUNCES STILTON CHEESE, RIND REMOVED, AT ROOM TEMPERATURE (*see* NOTE)

½ CUP SOUR CREAM

2 EGGS

2 TABLESPOONS HEAVY (WHIPPING) CREAM

TO PREPARE THE CANDIED WALNUTS, preheat the oven to 350°F and line a baking sheet with parchment paper or a nonstick baking mat. Put the port, sugar, and walnuts in a small saucepan over high heat and bring to a boil, stirring occasionally. Reduce the heat slightly and continue to cook until the port is very thick and syrupy, 10 to 15 minutes; be careful not to burn the port as it reduces. Remove the nuts from the pan with kitchen tongs or two forks and place them carefully on the prepared baking sheet; discard the port syrup. Place the baking sheet in the oven and toast the nuts until medium golden brown, 8 to 10 minutes. Remove the nuts from the oven, leaving the oven on for baking the crust; set the nuts aside.

TO PREPARE THE CRUST, line the bottom of a 6-by-3-inch springform pan or cake pan with aluminum foil and lightly oil or spray the sides of the pan with cooking spray. Put the crackers, ½ cup of the candied walnuts, the pepper, and melted butter in the bowl of a food processor fitted with a blade attachment. Process the mixture until the nuts are finely ground, about 30 seconds. Pour the crust into the prepared pan pressing firmly and evenly over the bottom. Put the pan into the oven and bake for 5 minutes. Remove the pan from the oven, place it on a cooling rack, and reduce the oven temperature to 300°F. Let the crust cool and then very carefully spread the fig jam on the baked crust with the back of a spoon. Set aside while preparing the filling.

CLEAN THE FOOD PROCESSOR bowl and blade attachment and put the cream cheese and Stilton inside the bowl. Process the mixture for 30 seconds and then scrape the sides of the bowl with a rubber spatula. Add the sour cream, eggs, and heavy cream. Process for another minute and scrape the bowl to make sure the mixture is smooth. Pour the filling evenly over the crust.

SET THE SPRINGFORM PAN in a slightly larger pan with 2- or 3-inch high sides to create a water bath. Center the pans in the oven and carefully fill the outer pan with hot water. Bake until the cheesecake jiggles slightly in the center when you shake it, about 1 hour. Remove the cake from the oven and carefully take the cake pan out of the water bath. Place it on a cooling rack, cool completely, and wrap with plastic film; refrigerate until completely cold, or overnight.

RUN A KNIFE around the rim of the springform pan, loosen the hinge, and then remove the ring carefully. Transfer the cake to a plate with the pan bottom in place.

If you have baked the cheesecake in a cake pan, have two plates larger than the cake ready to use. Place one plate on top of the pan and turn it upside down. Tap the pan on the counter to release the cake. Remove the pan and quickly remove the aluminum foil from the bottom. Place the other plate on top of the crust and invert so the cake is right-side up. Cut thin wedges with a sharp knife and serve garnished with the remaining candied walnuts.

NOTE

Fig jam or spread can be found in most specialty markets, but you can substitute Fig and Rosemary Spread (page 144) or another dark dried-fruit type of jam or spread.

Stilton cheese is an English blue cheese made from cow's milk. The texture is rich and creamy but slightly crumbly. It is commonly found in most supermarkets. Another type of blue cheese can be substituted for the Stilton, if desired.

NEW YORK-STYLE PARMIGIANO-REGGIANO CHEESECAKE

Everyone has a memory of thick, decadent New York–style cheesecake. I can almost taste the cake's velvety richness and the plump red cherries that crown its top. This rich, savory version uses the premium Parmesan cheese Parmigiano-Reggiano in its batter. The cheese adds a robust and distinct flavor to the creamy texture. Serve thin wedges with a lightly dressed salad, or enjoy crisp crostini spread with a little of the cake and serve as a cheese course.

CRUST

¾ CUP PLUS 2 TABLESPOONS WATER

¼ CUP CORNMEAL

½ TEASPOON SALT

¼ CUP FINELY GRATED PARMIGIANO-REGGIANO CHEESE *(see page 24)*

¾ CUP SLICED ALMONDS, TOASTED

FILLING

TWO 8-OUNCE PACKAGES CREAM CHEESE AT ROOM TEMPERATURE

1½ CUPS FINELY GRATED PARMIGIANO-REGGIANO CHEESE *(see page 24)*

½ CUP HEAVY (WHIPPING) CREAM

3 EGGS

½ CUP SOUR CREAM

TO PREPARE THE CRUST, line the bottom of a 6-by-3-inch springform pan or a cake pan with aluminum foil and lightly oil or spray the sides of the pan with cooking spray. Put the water in a small saucepan over high heat and bring to a boil. Reduce the heat to low and stir vigorously with a rubber spatula while adding the cornmeal. Cook and stir for 5 minutes. Remove the pan from the heat and stir in the salt, cheese, and almonds. Press the warm crust into the prepared pan and set aside.

MEANWHILE, PREPARE THE FILLING. Preheat the oven to 300°F. Put the cream cheese and grated cheese in the bowl of a food processor fitted with a blade attachment. Process for 30 seconds, scraping the sides of the bowl with a rubber spatula occasionally. Add the cream and process until smooth, about 15 seconds. Add the eggs one at a time, scraping the sides of the bowl between additions. Pour the filling evenly over the crust.

SET THE SPRINGFORM PAN inside a slightly larger pan with 2- or 3-inch-high sides to create a water bath. Center the pans in the oven and carefully fill the outer pan with hot water. Bake until the cheesecake jiggles slightly in the center when you shake it, about 1 hour. Remove the cake and water bath from the oven and place on a cooling rack.

STIR THE SOUR CREAM in a small bowl and then carefully spread it over the hot cheesecake. Return it to the oven, still in the water bath, and bake for an additional 10 minutes. Remove the cake and water bath from the oven and let sit on a cooling rack for 10 minutes. Take the cake out of the water bath carefully. Discard the water bath. Place the cake on a cooling rack, let cool completely, and then wrap with plastic film and refrigerate until completely cold, about 2 hours.

RUN A KNIFE around the rim of the springform pan, loosen the hinge, and then remove the ring carefully. Transfer the cake to a plate with the pan bottom in place. If you have baked the cheescake in a cake pan, have two plates, larger than the cake, ready to use. Place one plate on top of the pan and turn it upside down. Tap the pan on the counter to release the cake. Remove the pan and quickly peel the aluminum foil from the bottom. Place the other plate on top of the crust and invert so the cake is right-side up. Cut into thin wedges with a sharp knife. Any leftover cake can be wrapped and refrigerated for up to 1 week.

PORTOBELLO MUSHROOM, ROSEMARY, AND SHALLOT CREAM CLAFOUTI

A clafouti is a rustic dessert popular in Provence. It is usually made with black cherries blanketed with a thin, white sweet batter, baked, and served hot. My earthy and aromatic savory rendition is decadent, rich, and flavorful. It is delicious served with roasted meats or poultry. Mix and match mushrooms for fun, if you like.

CLAFOUTI BATTER

¼ CUP DRIED PORTOBELLO MUSHROOMS *(see Note)*

¾ CUP BOILING WATER

½ CUP ALL-PURPOSE FLOUR

¼ TEASPOON SALT

2 EGGS

FILLING

4 TABLESPOONS EXTRA-VIRGIN OLIVE OIL

8 OUNCES FRESH PORTOBELLO MUSHROOMS, STEMMED, THICKLY SLICED, AND CUT INTO 1-INCH CHUNKS

2 TABLESPOONS MINCED SHALLOTS

2 TEASPOONS FINELY CHOPPED FRESH ROSEMARY

1¼ CUPS HEAVY (WHIPPING) CREAM

½ TEASPOON SALT

¼ TEASPOON FRESHLY GROUND BLACK PEPPER

TO PREPARE THE BATTER, put the dried mushrooms in a small bowl and pour the boiling water over the top. Gently stir and then cover with plastic film. Let the mushrooms hydrate for 15 minutes. Drain, reserving ½ cup of the liquid. Chop the mushrooms into 1-inch pieces.

PUT THE FLOUR in a medium bowl. Pour the reserved mushroom liquid over the flour and whisk until smooth. Add the salt, eggs, and hydrated mushroom pieces. Continue mixing to a smooth batter.

MEANWHILE, PREPARE THE FILLING. Preheat the oven to 400°F. Lightly butter four shallow 6-ounce (¾-cup) ceramic dishes and arrange them on a baking sheet. Heat the olive oil in a large sauté pan or skillet over medium-high heat. Add the mushrooms and sauté until lightly browned on one side. Turn them over and brown the other side. Add the shallots and rosemary and continue to sauté until the shallots are translucent, about 1 minute. Stir in the heavy cream, salt, and pepper. Bring to a rapid boil and cook until the cream

is reduced by half, 1 to 2 minutes. Divide the mushroom cream among the prepared ceramic baking dishes.

POUR THE BATTER evenly over the mushroom cream and place the baking sheet in the oven. Bake until the crust looks puffed and the mushrooms are bubbling, about 15 minutes. Serve immediately from the oven.

NOTE

Although dried mushrooms are easy to find, not all varieties are available everywhere. Choose dried chanterelles or porcini, if you cannot find dried portobello mushrooms.

SOUFFLÉS

PÂTE
À CHOUX

POPOVERS

PASTRIES WITH PUFF

Puffy and light, these pastries are aerated by the power of eggs and high baking temperatures. Whisking popover ingredients together into a thin batter is as simple as making oatmeal. Soufflés make dramatic showstopping appetizers, entrées, or desserts. Profiteroles (miniature versions of cream puffs) and éclairs attribute their versatility to well-balanced basic ingredients that are transformed into elegant savory dishes of gougères and fritters, as well as sweet pastries that can be filled with creams and custards. Be inspired by these recipes and make a few of them your new favorites.

ORANGE-NUTMEG POPOVERS

Tall and stunning, these popovers make glorious, eye-pleasing presentations all by themselves! Airy and light, gently spiced with nutmeg, black pepper, and fresh orange peel, they are so simple to prepare, you'll want to make them a standard side dish. Spread with a little Apple, Pear, and Ginger Chutney (page 142) and serve next to soft scrambled eggs at breakfast or roasted pork tenderloin for dinner.

3 EGGS AT ROOM TEMPERATURE

I CUP WHOLE MILK AT ROOM TEMPERATURE

3 TABLESPOONS UNSALTED BUTTER, MELTED

I CUP ALL-PURPOSE FLOUR

I TEASPOON SALT

I TEASPOON DRIED OR FRESHLY GRATED NUTMEG

I TEASPOON FRESHLY GROUND BLACK PEPPER

ZEST OF I LARGE ORANGE

PUT THE EGGS, milk, and butter in a blender and mix on medium speed for 5 seconds. Add the flour, salt, nutmeg, pepper, and orange zest. Mix for another 15 seconds. Let the batter rest at room temperature for about 45 minutes.

PREHEAT THE OVEN to 375°F. Position a rack in the center of the oven, leaving 4 inches of space above the popover pan to allow plenty of unobstructed space for the popovers to rise. Put the popover pan on a baking sheet and place it in the oven for 2 minutes. Carefully remove the baking sheet from the oven and place it on a cooling rack. Quickly spray the inside of each deep cup with nonstick baking spray, and then pour the batter evenly among all six cups, filling each cup about two-thirds full.

CENTER THE BAKING SHEET back in the oven and bake the popovers until they are firm and golden brown on the outside, about 30 minutes. Do not open the oven door while they are cooking. Remove the baking sheet from the oven and prick each popover with a small knife to allow the steam to escape; this helps keep them from collapsing. Remove the popovers from each mold by carefully running a knife around the rim, gently twisting and pulling each out of the cup. Best served right from the oven.

POTATO CHEESE FRITTERS

Made with classic pâte à choux, cooked potatoes, and scallions, these fritters have a soft, pillowlike interior oozing with melted Jack cheese. The crispy crust adds lots of crunchiness. Enjoy them for a side dish or as an hors d'oeuvre with Smoky Tomato Sauce (page 152).

1 CUP WATER

2 TABLESPOONS UNSALTED BUTTER

1 TEASPOON SALT

¾ CUP ALL-PURPOSE FLOUR

2 EGGS

½ CUP RICED POTATO (ABOUT ½ OF A LARGE POTATO) *(see page 20)*

¼ CUP CHOPPED SCALLION, GREEN PART ONLY

2 CUPS JAPANESE BREAD CRUMBS (PANKO) FOR DIPPING

2 OUNCES MONTEREY JACK CHEESE, CUT INTO ½-INCH CUBES

6 CUPS (1½ QUARTS) VEGETABLE OR CANOLA OIL FOR FRYING

PUT THE WATER, butter, and salt into a 2-quart saucepan over medium heat. Bring to a rolling boil, then remove from the heat and add the flour. Stir vigorously with a wooden spoon until a ball forms. This will only take about 15 seconds. Return the saucepan to the heat and cook the mixture for another minute, stirring constantly.

TRANSFER THE DOUGH to the bowl of an electric mixer fitted with a paddle attachment and beat on medium speed to cool the dough, about 2 minutes. Add the eggs one at a time, incorporating the first one completely before adding the next. Scrape the sides of the bowl with a rubber spatula frequently. After both eggs are added, the dough should look thick and shiny and slowly fall from the spatula. Remove the dough from the mixer and stir in the potato and scallion until evenly mixed throughout the dough.

PUT THE BREAD CRUMBS in a small bowl. Using two spoons, carefully place a rounded tablespoon of the dough on top of the bread crumbs and press a cube of cheese into the center of the dough. Pull the dough up and over the cheese with the two spoons to completely conceal the cheese. Roll the fritter in the bread crumbs and place it on a baking sheet ready for frying. Each fritter should be about the size of a whole walnut. Continue until all of the fritters are stuffed with cheese and coated in bread crumbs.

HEAT THE OIL in a deep pan to 375°F (see page 24). Drop the fritters into the hot oil and fry for 2 to 3 minutes, then carefully turn over each one with tongs. Fry until both sides are golden brown. Remove, drain on paper towels, and serve while hot.

COCONUT SHRIMP FRITTERS WITH TROPICAL FRUIT RELISH

A slightly sweet coconut choux paste makes a delicious coating for shrimp. Coconut keeps the batter soft and chewy, while the outside turns golden and crisp when fried. Serve with Tropical Fruit Relish (page 146).

1 CUP LIGHT COCONUT MILK

3½ CUPS SHREDDED SWEETENED COCONUT

2 TABLESPOONS UNSALTED BUTTER

1 TEASPOON SALT

¾ CUP ALL-PURPOSE FLOUR

2 EGGS

12 JUMBO SHRIMP, DEVEINED, WITH TAILS ATTACHED

6 CUPS (1½ QUARTS) VEGETABLE OR CANOLA OIL FOR FRYING

COARSE SEA SALT FOR DUSTING

PUT THE COCONUT MILK, 1 cup of the shredded coconut, the butter, and salt in a 2-quart saucepan over medium-high heat. Bring to a rolling boil, then remove from the heat and add the flour. Stir vigorously with a wooden spoon until a ball forms. Return the saucepan to the burner and cook the mixture for another minute, stirring constantly.

TRANSFER THE DOUGH to the bowl of an electric mixer fitted with a paddle attachment and beat on medium speed to cool the dough, about 1 minute. Add the eggs one at a time, incorporating the first one completely before adding the next. Scrape the sides of the bowl with a rubber spatula frequently. After both eggs are added, the dough should look thick and shiny and fall from the spatula. Remove the dough from the mixer and place in a small bowl.

PUT THE REMAINING COCONUT in a medium bowl. Lay the shrimp on a paper towel and pat them very dry (this will help the batter stick to the shrimp). With two spoons, scoop out about 2 tablespoons of the dough and place on top of the coconut, spreading it out just a bit. Carefully lay one shrimp in the center of the dough. With the two spoons, pull the dough up over the shrimp to cover the shrimp but leave the tail hanging out. Coat both sides of the dough in coconut. Don't worry if the entire shrimp isn't covered in dough; the dough will expand and cover the shrimp as it cooks. Place the prepared coconut shrimp on a baking sheet. Continue until all the shrimp are coated with the dough and coconut. The coconut shrimp can be prepared early in the day and fried later the same day.

HEAT THE OIL in a deep pan to 350°F (see page 24) and preheat the oven to 300°F. Drop 2 to 3 shrimp at a time into the hot oil, fry for 2 to 3 minutes, then carefully turn over each puff with tongs. Fry until both sides are golden brown. Remove, drain on paper towels, and dust with coarse sea salt. Arrange the shrimp on a baking sheet and place it in the oven to keep the shrimp warm until all are fried. Arrange the fritters on a large serving platter.

CAPRESE SALAD–FILLED PROFITEROLES

I love the soft breadlike texture of these miniature basil cream puffs with the fresh tomatoes and mozzarella—the entire dish reminds me of a fresh summertime salad stuffed inside herb bread. Whip up this dish in just minutes by making and baking the profiteroles ahead of time. Serve as an appetizer or side dish, or serve larger puffs for a light lunch (see Note).

1 CUP WATER

3 TABLESPOONS UNSALTED BUTTER

½ TEASPOON SALT

1 TEASPOON DRIED BASIL

¾ CUP ALL-PURPOSE FLOUR

2 LARGE EGGS

¾ CUP (3 OUNCES) SHREDDED MOZZARELLA

1 RECIPE CAPRESE SALAD *(page 155)*

FRESH BASIL LEAVES FOR GARNISH

PREHEAT THE OVEN to 375°F and line the bottom of two baking sheets with parchment paper or nonstick baking mats. Put the water, butter, salt, and basil into a 2-quart saucepan over medium heat. Bring to a rolling boil, then remove from the heat and add the flour. Stir vigorously with a wooden spoon until a ball forms. This will only take about 15 seconds. Return the saucepan to the heat and cook the mixture for another minute, stirring constantly.

TRANSFER THE DOUGH to the bowl of an electric mixer fitted with a paddle attachment and beat on medium speed to cool the dough, about 2 minutes. Add the eggs one at a time, incorporating the first one completely before adding the next. Scrape the sides of the bowl frequently with a rubber spatula. After the eggs are added, the dough should look thick and shiny and fall easily from a rubber spatula. Remove the dough from the mixer and stir in the mozzarella.

USING TWO SPOONS, drop the dough in quarter-size dollops onto the baking sheets, leaving a good inch between each spoonful to allow the puffs room to expand while baking. Bake until puffed, double in size, and medium golden brown in color, 20 to 25 minutes. Transfer the baking sheets to racks for cooling (see *Note*).

USING A SMALL PARING KNIFE, cut off the top one-third of each profiterole. Fill the bottom two-thirds of each puff with a large spoonful of Caprese Salad. Garnish each with a fresh basil leaf, put the tops on, and arrange on a serving tray. Serve right away or refrigerate for up to 1 hour.

NOTE

For a light summer lunch, spoon the dough out in larger portions, about double the size, and bake for 30 to 35 minutes. Serve one filled puff in the center of a large plate and surround with greens tossed in olive oil and balsamic vinegar.

TOASTED CARAWAY AND
GRUYÈRE PUFFS

Gougères, classic French pastry puffs, are studded with Gruyère cubes that melt into tiny pockets of warm and puffy bites. You'll find it hard to say no to the last one left on the plate, especially if you serve them with warm Smoky Tomato Sauce (page 152).

1 TABLESPOON CARAWAY SEEDS, SLIGHTLY CRUSHED

1 CUP WATER

3 TABLESPOONS UNSALTED BUTTER

¼ TEASPOON SALT

1 CUP PLUS 2 TABLESPOONS UNBLEACHED ALL-PURPOSE FLOUR

3 LARGE EGGS

6 OUNCES GRUYÈRE, CUT INTO 1-INCH CUBES

PREHEAT THE OVEN to 375°F and line the bottom of two baking sheets with parchment paper or nonstick baking mats. Put the caraway seeds in a small nonstick skillet over medium heat. Stir and shake the pan until a fragrant smoke arises and the seeds are slightly darker, 2 to 3 minutes. Pour them into a small bowl and set aside.

PUT THE WATER, butter, and salt into a 2-quart saucepan over medium heat. Bring to a rolling boil, then remove from the heat and add the flour and caraway seeds. Stir vigorously with a wooden spoon until a ball forms. This will only take about 15 seconds. Return the saucepan to the heat and cook the mixture for another minute, stirring constantly.

TRANSFER THE DOUGH to the bowl of an electric mixer fitted with a paddle attachment and beat on medium speed to cool the dough, about 2 minutes. Add the eggs one at a time, incorporating each completely before adding the next. Scrape the sides of the bowl with a rubber spatula frequently. After all the eggs are added, the dough

should look thick and shiny and slowly fall from the spatula. Remove the dough from the mixer and stir in the cheese cubes.

USING TWO SPOONS, drop the dough in quarter-size dollops onto the baking sheets, leaving a good inch between each spoonful to allow the puffs room to expand while baking. Bake until puffed, double in size, and medium golden brown in color, 20 to 25 minutes. Pile the puffs on a serving platter and serve warm (see *Note*).

NOTE

It's best to bake the batter within 1 hour of making the dough, otherwise it starts to lose some of its puffing power as the eggs begin to weaken. Alternatively, the dough can be spooned out onto the baking sheet and placed in the freezer. After the dough pieces are completely frozen, put them in an airtight freezer bag and store in the freezer for up to 2 weeks. To bake, place the frozen puffs on 2 baking sheets lined with parchment paper or nonstick baking mats and thaw, then bake as directed.

SMOKED-BACON BEIGNETS

Try these light-textured pâte à choux–style beignets with loads of smoky bacon packed inside. Make the dough a day ahead, and they'll be ready to cook for breakfast or brunch or as an hors d'oeuvre dipped in Smoky Tomato Sauce (page 152).

1 CUP WATER

2 TABLESPOONS UNSALTED BUTTER

½ TEASPOON SALT

¾ CUP ALL-PURPOSE FLOUR

2 EGGS

10 STRIPS SMOKED BACON, COOKED CRISP AND CHOPPED INTO SMALL PIECES

6 CUPS (1½ QUARTS) VEGETABLE OIL OR CANOLA OIL FOR FRYING

PUT THE WATER, butter, and salt in a 2-quart saucepan and over medium heat, bring to a rolling boil, then remove from the heat and add the flour. Stir vigorously with a wooden spoon until a ball forms. This will only take about 15 seconds. Return the saucepan to the heat and cook the mixture for another minute, stirring constantly.

TRANSFER THE DOUGH to the bowl of an electric mixer fitted with a paddle attachment and beat on medium speed to cool the dough, about 2 minutes. Add the eggs one at a time, incorporating the first one completely before adding the next. Scrape the sides of the bowl frequently with a rubber spatula. After both eggs are added, the dough should look thick and shiny and

slowly fall from the spatula. Remove the dough from the mixer and stir in the bacon (see *Note*).

HEAT THE OIL in a deep pan to 375°F (see page 24). Drop rounded tablespoons of the batter into the hot oil, fry for 2 to 3 minutes, then carefully turn over each beignet with tongs. Fry until both sides are golden brown. Remove the beignets and drain on paper towels. Best served piping hot.

NOTE

The dough can be made several hours ahead and cooked to order. Spoon rounded tablespoons onto a baking sheet lined with parchment paper or a nonstick baking mat, cover, and refrigerate. Later, heat the oil and fry as directed.

SESAME ÉCLAIRS WITH HONEY-SOY ASPARAGUS

This recipe gives classic pâte à choux a fun Asian twist. Soy-glazed fresh asparagus peek out from inside sesame-studded éclairs. Save time by baking the éclairs ahead and freezing them for up to 1 week. Remove them from the freezer and place on a rack set on a baking sheet. When defrosted, put them in a preheated 425°F oven for 3 to 5 minutes to heat them through and crisp them up.

ÉCLAIRS

1½ CUPS WATER

¼ CUP (½ STICK) UNSALTED BUTTER

½ TEASPOON SALT

¼ TEASPOON FRESHLY GROUND BLACK PEPPER

1¼ CUPS ALL-PURPOSE FLOUR

4 EGGS, ONE OF THEM LIGHTLY BEATEN

1 TABLESPOON TOASTED SESAME SEEDS, PLUS MORE FOR SPRINKLING

ASPARAGUS

2 BUNCHES THIN ASPARAGUS, ABOUT 60 SPEARS

2 TEASPOONS CANOLA OIL OR ANY OTHER FLAVORLESS OIL

2 TEASPOONS LIGHT SESAME OIL

½ TEASPOON SALT

2 TEASPOONS MINCED PEELED FRESH GINGER

MARINADE

3 TABLESPOONS SOY SAUCE

2 TEASPOONS CLOVER HONEY

2 TEASPOONS LIGHT SESAME OIL

1 TEASPOON FRESH LEMON JUICE

2 TABLESPOONS TOASTED SESAME SEEDS

FILLING

6 OUNCES CREAM CHEESE AT ROOM TEMPERATURE

2 TEASPOONS SNIPPED CHIVES

2 TABLESPOONS HEAVY (WHIPPING) CREAM

¼ TEASPOON SALT

CONTINUED ➤

TO PREPARE THE ÉCLAIRS, preheat the oven to 375°F and line a baking sheet with parchment paper or a nonstick baking mat. Bring the water, butter, salt, and pepper to a rolling boil over medium heat. Remove from the heat and add the flour. Stir vigorously with a rubber spatula until a ball forms. This will only take about 15 seconds. Return the saucepan to the heat and cook the mixture for another minute, stirring constantly.

TRANSFER THE DOUGH to the bowl of an electric mixer fitted with a paddle attachment and beat on medium speed to cool the dough, about 2 minutes. Add 3 of the eggs one at a time, incorporating each completely before adding the next. Scrape the sides of the bowl with a rubber spatula frequently. After all 3 eggs are added, the dough should look thick and shiny and slowly fall from the spatula. Remove the dough from the mixer and stir in the sesame seeds.

FIT A 12- OR 14-INCH PIPING BAG with a 1-inch round piping tip and fill half full with the dough. Pipe 2-inch lengths of dough onto the cookie sheet, spacing them about 1 inch apart to allow room for expanding. Lightly brush the tops with a little of the beaten egg and sprinkle with more sesame seeds. Bake until golden brown, about 30 minutes. Do not open the oven until the éclairs are set and have lost their shine, or they may collapse. Transfer to a rack to cool.

TO PREPARE THE MARINADE, combine the soy sauce, honey, sesame oil, lemon juice, and sesame seeds in a large bowl and stir well to combine; set aside while preparing the asparagus.

WASH, TRIM, AND DRY the asparagus spears. Heat the canola and sesame oils in a large sauté pan or skillet over medium heat. Add the prepared asparagus along with the salt. Stir to coat the asparagus in oil. Cover with a lid and cook for 3 minutes. Remove the lid and stir in the ginger. Continue to sauté, stirring frequently, until the asparagus are tender but not overcooked, 3 to 5 minutes. Transfer the asparagus to the marinade and gently stir to coat. Chill for at least 30 minutes or overnight.

TO PREPARE THE FILLING, with a hand mixer or a stand mixer fitted with a paddle attachment, beat the cream cheese, chives, cream, and salt until soft and smooth, about 3 minutes.

CUT THE MARINATED asparagus into 2-inch lengths. Using a serrated knife, slice the éclairs in half lengthwise. Spread a thin layer of the chive cream cheese on each éclair half. Place six pieces of asparagus on one éclair half and cover with another. Repeat with the remaining éclair halves. Arrange the éclairs on a large serving plate and serve immediately or refrigerate for up to 1 hour; the éclairs will become soggy after that.

CAULIFLOWER AND PANCETTA PUFFED CRÊPES

This recipe lets you master the techniques of making crêpes and making soufflé batter. The light and puffy soufflé crêpes are loaded with the flavors of Italian bacon mingling with mild roasted cauliflower and cheese. Serve them for brunch or a light lunch. To save time, make and cook the crêpes and roast the cauliflower a day ahead.

CRÊPES

1 CUP ALL-PURPOSE FLOUR

¾ TEASPOON SALT

¾ CUP WHOLE MILK

2 EGGS

2 TABLESPOONS UNSALTED BUTTER, MELTED

ROASTED CAULIFLOWER

½ HEAD OF A SMALL CAULIFLOWER (¾ TO 1 POUND), TRIMMED AND CUT INTO 1-INCH FLORETS

2 TABLESPOONS EXTRA-VIRGIN OLIVE OIL

2 OUNCES PANCETTA, CUT INTO ¼-INCH PIECES

¼ TEASPOON SALT

½ CUP WATER

SOUFFLÉ FILLING

2 TABLESPOONS ALL-PURPOSE FLOUR

¼ TEASPOON SALT

⅓ CUP WHOLE MILK

½ CUP (2 OUNCES) SHREDDED MOZZARELLA CHEESE

1 TABLESPOON UNSALTED BUTTER

3 EGG YOLKS

4 EGG WHITES

¼ CUP DRY BREAD CRUMBS MIXED WITH 1 TABLESPOON MELTED BUTTER

TO PREPARE THE CRÊPES, stir the flour and salt together in a small bowl. Put the milk, eggs, and melted butter in a blender and blend for a few seconds. Add the flour and blend until completely smooth, about 15 seconds. Let the crêpe batter rest for half an hour.

LINE A TRAY with parchment paper. Heat a crêpe pan or a 7-inch nonstick sauté pan or skillet over moderately high heat. Spray the pan lightly with cooking oil or brush with melted butter. Pour ¼ cup of batter into the sides of the pan and swirl to coat the bottom, forming a thin layer. Cook until bubbles appear on the surface of the

crêpe and the edges begin to brown lightly. Flip the crêpe over using a spatula. Cook the second side for about 10 seconds, then turn the crêpe onto the prepared tray to cool. Continue cooking crêpes until all the batter is used. You should have 6 crêpes.

TO ROAST THE CAULIFLOWER, preheat the oven to 425°F. Toss the cauliflower with the olive oil, pancetta, and salt. Spread the mixture over the bottom of a baking pan and roast for 30 minutes, tossing the cauliflower halfway through baking. Remove the baking pan from the oven, pour water over the cauliflower, and cover with

CONTINUED ➤

aluminum foil. Place back in the oven for another 15 minutes or until fork-tender. Remove from the oven and place on a cooling rack, leaving the oven at 425°F.

TO PREPARE THE SOUFFLÉ FILLING, lightly butter a 9-by-13-inch baking dish. Put the flour and salt into a small bowl and add half of the milk. Whisk until smooth. Continue to whisk while adding the remaining milk and the cheese. Put the butter in a small saucepan and melt over medium heat. Pour the milk mixture over the melted butter and whisk continuously. Bring to a light boil and mix for 15 seconds. Pour the mix into a large bowl and stir in the cauliflower. Whisk for 1 minute to cool the mixture, then blend in the egg yolks.

POUR THE EGG WHITES into the bowl of an electric mixer fitted with the whip attachment. Whip at medium speed until the egg whites form shiny, medium peaks that hold their shape. Gently fold the egg whites into the cauliflower mixture. Lay all the crêpes out on the counter and scoop about $1/3$ cup batter onto half of each crêpe. Fold each crêpe over its batter forming a half-moon shape. Shingle the crêpes into the bottom of the baking dish, overlapping slightly, and then sprinkle with the buttered bread crumbs. Put the baking dish into the oven and bake until the crêpes are puffed and brown around the edges, about 15 minutes. Serve while hot and puffy.

SHIITAKE MUSHROOM AND GARLIC SOUFFLÉS

Rich, meaty mushrooms and toasted garlic make these moist soufflés memorable. Serve as a side dish with most meat and fish dishes or as a light entrée with warm Smoky Tomato Sauce (page 152).

FILLING

3 TABLESPOONS EXTRA-VIRGIN OLIVE OIL

6 OUNCES SHIITAKE MUSHROOMS, CHOPPED

2 LARGE GARLIC CLOVES, MINCED

SALT AND FRESHLY GROUND BLACK PEPPER

SOUFFLÉ BASE

3 TABLESPOONS UNBLEACHED ALL-PURPOSE FLOUR

¾ CUP WHOLE MILK

2 TABLESPOONS UNSALTED BUTTER

3 LARGE EGG YOLKS

5 LARGE EGG WHITES AT ROOM TEMPERATURE

TO PREPARE THE FILLING, heat the olive oil in a large sauté pan or skillet over medium heat. Add the mushrooms and sauté until golden on one side. Turn the mushrooms over, sprinkle the garlic on top, and season to taste with salt and pepper. Sauté the mushrooms and garlic until golden brown, about 1 minute. Remove the mushrooms from the pan. Set aside while preparing the soufflé base.

TO PREPARE THE SOUFFLÉ base, put the flour into a small bowl, add half of the milk, and whisk smooth. Continue to whisk while adding the remaining milk. Put the butter in a small saucepan and melt over medium heat. Pour the milk

mixture over the melted butter and whisk continuously. Bring to a light boil and continue whisking for 15 seconds. Pour the mix into a large bowl and stir in the sautéed mushrooms. Whisk for 1 minute to cool the mixture slightly, then blend in the egg yolks.

PREHEAT THE OVEN to 400°F and lightly butter the sides and bottoms of four 8-ounce (1-cup) ceramic ramekins and arrange them on a baking sheet. Pour the egg whites into the bowl of an electric mixer fitted with the whip attachment. Whip at medium speed until the egg whites form shiny, medium peaks that hold their shape. Stir half of the whites into the soufflé base

to lighten it. Fold in the remaining whites and spoon the soufflé mixture evenly among the ramekins (see *Note*).

BAKE UNTIL THE SOUFFLÉS are just set in the center and golden on top, about 15 minutes. To test for doneness, use a paring knife to pry the top of a soufflé open and look inside; it should appear softly set. Serve immediately after removing from the oven.

NOTE

A soufflé baked in one large ceramic mold looks stunning and makes a great family-style meal. This recipe will fill one 1-quart (4-cup) ceramic ramekin. Reduce the oven temperature to 350°F and bake for 35 to 45 minutes.

WINTER SQUASH, BROWN BUTTER, AND SAGE SOUFFLÉS

Choose from a variety of winter squash with a sweet taste and velvety flesh. I love the delicate flavor and smooth texture of acorn, kabocha, butternut, and hubbard squash. The brown butter adds an accent of nuttiness to the squash. A dusting of Parmesan cheese crowns each soufflé with a splash of pizzazz!

1 MEDIUM WINTER SQUASH (ABOUT 2 POUNDS)

¼ CUP CHICKEN BROTH

½ CUP FINELY GRATED PARMESAN CHEESE *(see page 24)*, PLUS MORE FOR DUSTING AND FOR GARNISH

1 TABLESPOON DRIED SAGE

¾ TEASPOON SALT

3 EGG YOLKS

3 TABLESPOONS ALL-PURPOSE FLOUR

¾ CUP WHOLE MILK

6 TABLESPOONS UNSALTED BUTTER

4 EGG WHITES AT ROOM TEMPERATURE

PREHEAT THE OVEN to 375°F. Put the squash on a cutting board and carefully cut it in half lengthwise with a large chef's knife or serrated knife. Poke 2 or 3 slits into the squash skin and place the two halves, flesh-side down, on a baking sheet. Roast until tender to the touch, about 30 minutes. Remove from the oven and let cool (see Note).

SCOOP OUT the seeds with a spoon and discard them. Carefully scoop out the cooked flesh. Place half in a blender with the chicken broth and blend until smooth. You should have about ½ cup of purée. Pour the purée into a large bowl; add the cheese, sage, salt, and egg yolks and whisk until smooth. Cut the remaining squash into

½-inch chunks and fold them into the puréed mixture. Set aside.

PREHEAT THE OVEN to 400°F. Lightly butter the sides and bottoms of six 6-ounce (¾ cup) ceramic ramekins and dust them with grated Parmesan cheese. Arrange the ramekins on a baking sheet and set aside.

PUT THE FLOUR in a small bowl and add the milk slowly while whisking. Whisk until completely smooth. Put the butter in a medium saucepan and melt over medium heat. Simmer the butter while stirring constantly, until it looks brown and smells toasty, about 1 minute.

CONTINUED ➤

Remove from the heat and whisk the flour-and-milk mixture into the butter. Place the saucepan back on the stove and cook for 30 seconds. Pour into the squash mixture and whisk together.

POUR THE EGG WHITES into the bowl of an electric mixer fitted with the whip attachment. Whip at medium speed until the egg whites form shiny, medium peaks that hold their shape. Stir half of the whites into the squash base to lighten it. Fold in the remaining whites and spoon the soufflé mixture evenly among the buttered ramekins. Sprinkle each soufflé with grated Parmesan cheese.

IMMEDIATELY PLACE the soufflés into the oven and bake until they are just set in the center and golden on top, 15 to 20 minutes. To test for doneness, use a paring knife to pry the top of a soufflé open just enough to look inside; it should appear softly set. Serve immediately after removing from the oven.

NOTE

Roast your squash 1 or 2 days beforehand, if you like. Wrap and store in the refrigerator until you are ready to assemble and bake the soufflés.

TOMATO-BASIL SOUFFLÉ

Moist tomatoes help these soufflés stay soft and tender. A little lemon juice brightens the natural tomato flavor. I like using chopped fresh or prepared tomatoes better than tomato paste because of the great texture they give the soufflé. Serve hot out of the oven with a side of warm Smoky Tomato Sauce (page 152) as a first course or as a side dish or, in slightly larger portions, for an entrée.

3 TABLESPOONS ALL-PURPOSE FLOUR

¾ CUP WHOLE MILK

3 TABLESPOONS UNSALTED BUTTER

¾ CUP CHOPPED TOMATOES, DRAINED (*see* Note)

¾ CUP (3 OUNCES) SHREDDED FRESH MOZZARELLA

I TABLESPOON PLUS 2 TEASPOONS CHOPPED FRESH BASIL

I TEASPOON FRESH LEMON JUICE

SALT AND FRESHLY GROUND BLACK PEPPER

4 EGG YOLKS

4 LARGE EGG WHITES AT ROOM TEMPERATURE

PREHEAT THE OVEN to 375°F. Lightly butter the sides and bottoms of four 6-ounce (¾-cup) ceramic ramekins and place them on a baking sheet. Whisk the flour in a small bowl and add half of the milk. Continue to whisk while adding the remaining milk. Melt the butter in a small saucepan over medium heat. Pour the milk mixture over the butter and bring it to a light boil while whisking continuously for 15 seconds. Pour into a large bowl and stir in the chopped tomatoes, mozzarella, and basil. Stir in the lemon juice and season to taste with salt and pepper. Blend in the egg yolks.

POUR THE EGG WHITES into the bowl of an electric mixer fitted with a whip attachment. Whip at medium speed until the egg whites form shiny peaks that hold their shape. Stir half of the whipped whites into the tomato base to lighten it. Fold in the remaining whites and spoon the soufflé mixture evenly among the buttered ramekins. The soufflé batter should fill the molds to the top.

BAKE THE SOUFFLÉS on a baking sheet until they are just set in the center and golden on top, about 20 minutes; do not open the oven door while baking. To test for doneness, use a paring knife to pry the top of a soufflé open and look inside; it should appear softly set. Serve hot from the oven.

NOTE

Canned chopped and drained tomatoes or Pomi tomatoes in Tetra Paks can be substituted for the fresh tomatoes in this recipe.

SOFT

CRISPY

CHEWY

FLAKY

COOKIES

Cookies come in endless shapes, sizes, and flavors. Six basic shaping methods give the different types of cookies their names. Rolled cookies are made by rolling out a stiff dough mixture with a rolling pin and then cutting them into desired shapes and sizes. Piped cookies, or spritz, are made by forcing stiff dough through a pastry bag. Dropped cookies are made by scooping out a portion of the dough with a spoon and then dropping the cookies onto a baking sheet. Sheet cookies are spread over the entire baking sheet, baked, and cut into bars or squares. Icebox cookies are formed into a round log, which can be prepared in advance and held in the refrigerator until needed; then they are thinly sliced. Molded cookies are thin, crispy wafers shaped over a container to give them a curved form. Whether one shape or several shapes, a variety of cookies makes an appealing treat for the eye. The savory cookies in this chapter are created using many of the shaping methods and they have their own distinct flavor characteristics.

THYME, LEMON, AND SEA-SALT SHORTBREAD

Tender and crisp, packed with delicate herbal and aromatic lemon flavors, these rolled shortbread cookies accented with a little sea salt are easy to prepare, versatile, and delicious.

1¾ CUPS ALL-PURPOSE FLOUR

¼ TEASPOON SALT

1 TABLESPOON FRESHLY GRATED LEMON ZEST

1½ TEASPOONS FINELY CHOPPED FRESH THYME

½ CUP (1 STICK) UNSALTED BUTTER AT ROOM TEMPERATURE

1 LARGE EGG, LIGHTLY BEATEN

2 LARGE EGG YOLKS

2 TEASPOONS WATER

1 TABLESPOON COARSE SEA SALT

STIR THE FLOUR, salt, lemon zest, and thyme together in a medium bowl. Add the butter and work it into the flour mixture until a coarse, crumbly mixture forms. Blend the lightly beaten egg, egg yolks, and water together. Reserve 1 tablespoon of the egg mixture for brushing.

MAKE A WELL in the center of the flour mixture. Add the egg mixture and blend together with your hands without kneading the dough together; the dough will look a bit crumbly. Turn the dough out onto a lightly floured work surface. Knead the dough together once or twice, just until it sticks together. Press the dough into a 1-inch-thick disc, wrap in plastic film, and refrigerate until firm, about 30 minutes.

PREHEAT THE OVEN to 350°F and line the bottom of a baking sheet with parchment paper or a nonstick baking mat. Remove the dough from the refrigerator, unwrap, and place it on a floured work surface. Press the dough into a 6-by-5-inch rectangle. With a rolling pin, roll the dough into a larger 10-by-7-inch rectangle, about ¼ inch thick. Cut the dough in half, forming two 5-by-7-inch pieces. Using a pizza wheel or sharp paring knife, cut crosswise into ½-inch-wide strips. Carefully place the cookies on the prepared baking sheet leaving a little room between each cookie. Brush the tops with the reserved egg mixture and sprinkle a little coarse sea salt on top. Gently press the salt into the surface of each cookie so it does not fall off. Bake until lightly browned, about 20 minutes. Transfer to a cooling rack and serve warm or at room temperature. Store the cookies in an airtight container at room temperature for up to 1 week.

CRISPY POTATO HAYSTACKS

Call these cookies or call them snacks! I call them macaroon haystack takeoffs that take only minutes to make. Serve warm right out of the oven and enjoy the crisp, chewy, cheesy, and spicy sensations of each bite.

1¼ CUPS (ONE 1.7-OUNCE CAN) CRISP POTATO STICKS

1 EGG WHITE

1 TEASPOON RED PEPPER FLAKES

½ CUP FINELY GRATED PARMESAN CHEESE *(see page 24)*

¾ CUP (3 OUNCES) SHREDDED MOZZARELLA

PREHEAT THE OVEN to 375°F and line a baking sheet with parchment paper or a nonstick baking mat. Put the potato sticks in a medium bowl. Add the egg white and toss until the potato sticks are evenly coated. Sprinkle with the red pepper flakes, Parmesan, and mozzarella.

USING YOUR HANDS, divide the mixture into twelve mounds on the prepared baking sheet, piling them high as you work. Wash your hands, then press each haystack firmly with your fingertips so the potato sticks within the stacks stick together.

PLACE IN THE OVEN and bake until the haystacks are golden brown, about 10 minutes. These cookies are best served right out of the oven.

PECAN THUMBPRINTS

These rich pecan cookies taste great with a variety of fillings. Be creative with your filling choices and savor them as they melt in your mouth. For a pleasing sweet and savory combination, fill each cookie with Apple, Pear, and Ginger Chutney (page 142) or Fig and Rosemary Spread (page 144).

2 CUPS ALL-PURPOSE FLOUR

1 CUP PECAN PIECES, TOASTED AND ROUGHLY CHOPPED

1 CUP UNSALTED BUTTER AT ROOM TEMPERATURE

1 TABLESPOON PLUS 1 TEASPOON GRANULATED SUGAR

1 TEASPOON SALT

PREHEAT THE OVEN to 350°F. Blend the flour and pecans together in a small bowl. Put the butter, sugar, and salt in the bowl of an electric mixer fitted with a paddle attachment. Beat at medium speed for 1 minute, scraping down the sides of the bowl once or twice. Add the flour mixture and blend until the ingredients come together.

ROLL A SLIGHTLY heaping teaspoonful of dough into a ball and place it on an ungreased baking sheet. Gently press a finger into the center of the dough to make an indentation large enough to hold about a teaspoon of filling. Continue making cookies until all the dough is used, spacing them slightly apart. Bake the cookies until they are very light brown around the edges, about 12 minutes.

TRANSFER TO A RACK TO COOL. When completely cool, spoon about a teaspoon of filling of your choice in the center of each cookie. Store unfilled cookies in an airtight container for up to 4 days and filled cookies for up to 2 days.

TARRAGON-TOMATO STRIPES

The color and flavor of these pretty cookies are complemented with tarragon and naturally sweet tomato. Dip them in a little Tapenade Cream (page 145), or serve with a Cheddar cheese spread.

TARRAGON DOUGH

6 TABLESPOONS UNSALTED BUTTER AT ROOM TEMPERATURE

I TEASPOON GRANULATED SUGAR

½ TEASPOON SALT

I TABLESPOON PLUS I TEASPOON DRIED TARRAGON

I EGG AT ROOM TEMPERATURE

I EGG YOLK AT ROOM TEMPERATURE

I CUP PLUS 2 TABLESPOONS ALL-PURPOSE FLOUR

TOMATO DOUGH

¼ CUP UNSALTED BUTTER AT ROOM TEMPERATURE

⅓ CUP TOMATO PASTE

½ TEASPOON BALSAMIC VINEGAR

½ TEASPOON GRANULATED SUGAR

½ TEASPOON SALT

I EGG WHITE

I CUP ALL-PURPOSE FLOUR

I EGG WHITE FOR BRUSHING

TO PREPARE THE TARRAGON dough, put the butter, sugar, salt, and tarragon in the bowl of an electric mixer fitted with a paddle attachment or a food processor fitted with a blade attachment. Beat on high speed until light and creamy, about 2 minutes. Scrape the sides of the bowl and add the egg and egg yolk. Beat until creamy and smooth, about 3 minutes. The mixture may look separated but don't worry; as you keep mixing, it will soon become smooth. Add the flour and blend just until the dough comes together in a mass. Press the dough into a 1-inch-thick disc, wrap tightly in plastic film, and refrigerate until the dough is chilled and somewhat firm, 45 to 60 minutes.

TO PREPARE THE TOMATO dough, clean the bowl and the paddle attachment and put the butter, tomato paste, balsamic vinegar, sugar, and salt in the bowl. Beat until creamy, about 1 minute. Scrape the sides of the bowl and beat until creamy and smooth, another minute. Add the egg white and blend smooth, about 1 minute. Add the flour and blend just until the dough comes together in a mass. Press the dough into a 1-inch-thick disc, and wrap tightly in plastic film, and refrigerate until the dough is chilled and somewhat firm, 45 to 60 minutes.

UNWRAP THE TARRAGON DOUGH and place it on a floured work surface. Form the dough into a small rectangle with your hands. Dust the top of the dough with flour and gently roll it into a 10-by-7-inch rectangle, about ¼ inch thick. Place the dough onto a baking sheet and refrigerate.

CONTINUED ➤

UNWRAP THE TOMATO DOUGH and roll it into a 10-by-7-inch rectangle about ¼ inch thick. Remove the baking sheet with the tarragon dough from the refrigerator. Brush the top surface with a little of the egg white. Carefully pick up the tomato dough and place it on top of the tarragon dough. Cut the sandwiched dough in half to make two 5-by-7-inch rectangles. Brush one rectangle with egg white and carefully place the other on top, creating four alternating layers of tomato dough and tarragon dough. Place a piece of plastic film over the layered dough and refrigerate until firm, about 1 hour (see *Note*).

PREHEAT THE OVEN to 375°F. Remove the chilled dough from the refrigerator and place it on a cutting board. Using a sharp knife, cut the dough crosswise into 1¾-inch bars. Cut each bar into ¼-inch slices. Space the cookies slightly apart on two ungreased baking sheets and bake until the cookies have just a little color underneath (they will not be brown on top), 6 to 8 minutes. Be careful not to overbake the cookies, or they will lose their flavor and taste bitter and dry. Remove the cookies from the oven to cool. Store in an airtight container at room temperature for up to 3 days.

NOTE

Once the dough layers are assembled, they can be wrapped in plastic film and frozen for up to 1 month. To thaw and bake, remove the dough from the freezer and place in the refrigerator for 2 hours. Unwrap, slice the remaining cookies, and bake as directed.

ROSEMARY FRUIT BISCOTTI

These classic twice-baked Italian cookies are sweetened with dried fruits and seasoned with a hint of rosemary. Try a little Fig and Rosemary Spread (page 144) on top and serve with a salad.

2 CUPS ALL-PURPOSE FLOUR

2 TABLESPOONS GRANULATED SUGAR

½ TEASPOON BAKING POWDER

¼ TEASPOON BAKING SODA

¼ TEASPOON SALT

3 TABLESPOONS FINELY CHOPPED FRESH ROSEMARY

½ CUP (2 OUNCES) SLICED ALMONDS, TOASTED

½ CUP DRIED CHERRIES

½ CUP RAISINS

2 EGGS

2 EGG WHITES

3 TABLESPOONS COLD WATER

1 EGG YOLK FOR BRUSHING

COARSE SEA SALT

PREHEAT THE OVEN to 350°F and line a baking sheet with parchment paper or a nonstick baking mat. Toss the flour, sugar, baking powder, baking soda, salt, rosemary, sliced almonds, cherries, and raisins together in a large bowl to blend the ingredients together. Whisk the eggs, egg whites, and water together in a small bowl. Pour the egg mixture over the flour mixture and blend together briefly with your hands to form a dough.

PUT THE DOUGH on a lightly floured surface, knead 3 to 4 times, then divide the dough into 2 equal pieces. Gently roll each piece into a 10-inch-long log. Place the logs on the baking sheet, spacing them at least 2 inches apart. Brush the tops of each log lightly with egg yolk and dust with coarse sea salt. Gently press the salt into the logs so it doesn't fall off.

BAKE UNTIL THE LOGS are lightly browned, about 20 minutes. Transfer to a rack to cool slightly. Reduce the oven temperature to 300°F. Put one of the biscotti logs on a cutting board. Using a sharp serrated knife and a long sawing motion, cut the log into ⅛-inch-thick slices. Repeat with the remaining logs. Put each cookie back on the baking sheet and bake for 10 minutes. Turn each cookie over and bake for another 10 minutes. Let cool on a rack completely and then store in an airtight container at room temperature for up to 2 weeks.

SOUR CREAM FIG SPIRALS

MAKES

3

DOZEN

*Sweet and savory, orange-scented whole-wheat spirals pair nicely with Fig and Rosemary Spread (page 144).
Serve with thin slices of hard cheese for snacks or bring out a tray at your next cocktail party. Make the
dough several days ahead and refrigerate until you're ready to roll and assemble.*

1 CUP WHOLE-WHEAT FLOUR

½ CUP WALNUTS, TOASTED AND FINELY GROUND

¼ TEASPOON SALT

¼ CUP UNSALTED BUTTER AT ROOM TEMPERATURE

2 OUNCES CREAM CHEESE AT ROOM TEMPERATURE

ZEST OF 1 ORANGE

¼ CUP SOUR CREAM OR CRÈME FRAÎCHE *(page 149)*

1 EGG

⅓ CUP FIG AND ROSEMARY SPREAD *(page 144)*

GENEROUSLY DUST a large piece of plastic film with flour and set aside. Blend the flour, walnuts, and salt together in a small bowl. Put the butter, cream cheese, and orange zest in the bowl of an electric mixer fitted with a paddle attachment. Beat at medium speed until creamy, about 1 minute. Scrape the sides of the bowl, and then add the sour cream. Beat for another minute. Add the egg and beat until smooth. Add the flour mixture and mix just until the ingredients come together into a dough.

REMOVE THE DOUGH from the mixer and place it in the center of the flour-dusted plastic film. Dust the top of the dough with flour, then form it into a small rectangle. Gently press or roll the dough with a rolling pin into an 8-by-12-inch rectangle ¼ inch thick. Using an offset spatula, spread the fig jam carefully over the dough, spreading all the way to the edges.

ROLL THE DOUGH into a spiral starting at the long side of the rectangle farthest away from you. Tuck ½ inch of the dough's edge tightly over the filling, then begin to roll toward you, using the plastic film to help form a tight roll. Wrap the cookie spiral in plastic film and refrigerate for several hours until firm enough to cut, or overnight.

PREHEAT THE OVEN to 350°F and line a baking sheet with parchment paper or a nonstick baking mat. Remove the cookie spiral from the refrigerator, unwrap, and place it on a cutting board. Using a small knife, cut into ¼-inch-thick slices and place them on the prepared baking sheet. Bake until the cookies are just beginning to brown, 12 to 15 minutes. Transfer to a rack for cooling.

STORE THE COOKIES in an airtight container at room temperature for up to 1 week. Make the cookie spiral ahead and freeze it for up to 1 month. Remove the spiral from the freezer and put it in the refrigerator for several hours to thaw. Slice and bake as directed.

ITALIAN-SCENTED MADELEINES

Better make a double batch of these delicate and airy little cakes—they'll go fast!

1½ TEASPOON ITALIAN SEASONING

½ CUP ALL-PURPOSE FLOUR

3 TABLESPOONS YELLOW CORNMEAL

½ TEASPOON BAKING POWDER

½ CUP FINELY GRATED PARMESAN CHEESE *(see page 24)*

2 EGGS AT ROOM TEMPERATURE

1 TABLESPOON GRANULATED SUGAR

¾ TEASPOON SALT

3 TABLESPOONS UNSALTED BUTTER, MELTED AND COOLED

PREHEAT THE OVEN to 375°F and spray the indentations of one tray of 24 tiny madeleine molds with nonstick cooking spray, then sprinkle the inside of each with a little Italian seasoning. Sift the flour, cornmeal, and baking powder into a medium bowl and then stir in the cheese.

PUT THE EGGS, sugar, and salt in the bowl of an electric mixer fitted with a whip attachment. Whip on medium-high until the mixture is thick and foamy, 5 to 8 minutes. Gently but quickly, fold in the flour mixture using a spatula. Fold in the butter. The batter will be glossy, smooth, and homogeneous.

FIT A ½-INCH metal pastry tip into a 12- or 14-inch pastry bag and fill the pastry bag half full with batter. Pipe batter into each mold, filling them halfway. Place the pan into the oven and bake until the cakes are pale yellow and puffed and spring back when lightly touched in the centers, 4 to 6 minutes. To help the tiny cakes retain their moisture, do not leave them in the oven to brown. Remove the pan from the oven and invert the pan, gently tapping the corner on a work surface to release each cake. Store in an airtight container as soon as they cool. Best eaten within a day.

FIVE-SPICE BLACK-AND-WHITE SESAME WAFERS

These crisp wafers with loads of black and white sesame seeds and a warm, spiced Asian flair look pretty and taste great. Try serving Apple, Pear, and Ginger Chutney (page 142) on top of each or crumble the wafers over a Chinese chicken salad.

¼ CUP WHITE SESAME SEEDS

¼ CUP BLACK SESAME SEEDS

3 TABLESPOONS ALL-PURPOSE FLOUR

¼ TEASPOON SALT

I TABLESPOON CHINESE FIVE-SPICE POWDER

4 EGG WHITES

PREHEAT THE OVEN to 350°F and line a 17-by-12-inch baking sheet with a nonstick baking mat. Put the white and black sesame seeds, flour, salt, and five-spice powder in a medium bowl and stir together. Whisk in the egg whites until well blended. Using an offset spatula, spread the batter very thinly and evenly on the baking mat, covering about three-fourths of the surface. Put the baking sheet in the oven and bake until the wafer is brown on top, about 10 minutes. Remove the baking sheet to a cooling rack and carefully invert the baking mat. Peel the mat away from the wafer. Put the baking sheet and wafer, bottom-side up, back in the oven for another 10 minutes. Both sides of the wafer will be well browned. Let the wafer cool, then break it into large odd-size pieces. Store the wafer pieces airtight at room temperature for up to 1 week.

BLACK-RIMMED PISTACHIO WAFERS

This green icebox cookie looks stunning and tastes great plain or with cheese, fruit, or other condiments. Make the dough any time (see Note*), and you'll be ready to bake them fresh when you like.*

½ CUP DRY-ROASTED PISTACHIOS, PLUS MORE FOR GARNISH

¼ CUP (½ STICK) UNSALTED BUTTER AT ROOM TEMPERATURE

I TEASPOON GRANULATED SUGAR

½ TEASPOON SALT

2 EGGS, ONE OF THEM SEPARATED

¾ CUP ALL-PURPOSE FLOUR

½ CUP BLACK POPPY SEEDS

PUT THE PISTACHIOS, butter, sugar, and salt in the bowl of a food processor fitted with a blade attachment. Process until the nuts are the size of meal, about 2 minutes, scraping the bowl several times. Add 1 egg and the yolk of the separated egg and process until smooth, another 2 minutes. Add the flour and pulse just until the mixture forms a single mass.

TURN THE DOUGH out onto an unfloured work surface and press it into a log about 7 inches long. Brush a little of the egg white over the entire outside surface of the log. Pour the poppy seeds onto a large plate or clean work surface. Roll the log in the poppy seeds, making sure to coat the outside completely by pressing the seeds gently into the log. Wrap the cookie log in plastic film and refrigerate until firm, about 2 hours, or overnight (see *Note*).

PREHEAT THE OVEN to 375°F. Remove the cookie log from the refrigerator and place it on a cutting board. Using a small, sharp knife, cut into thin slices, about ⅛ inch thick; put the slices spaced slightly apart on a baking sheet. Dab a little egg white in the center of each cookie and top with a pistachio. Bake until very light brown, 5 to 6 minutes. (Be sure not to overbake or the pistachios will lose their delicate, nutty flavor.) Remove from the oven and let cool on a rack. Store the cookies in an airtight container at room temperature for up to 3 days.

NOTE

The prepared cookie log can be wrapped airtight and frozen for up to 1 month before baking. Thaw in the refrigerator for 3 hours, then slice and bake as directed.

APRICOT-FLECKED
GOAT CHEESE STRAWS

Goat cheese adds a creamy texture and mild flavor to these apricot-filled, sweet and tangy cookies. Serve an assortment of savory cookies for a special occasion and enjoy the pleasing response.

1½ CUPS SLICED BLANCHED ALMONDS

¼ CUP (½ STICK) UNSALTED BUTTER AT ROOM TEMPERATURE

4 OUNCES FRESH GOAT CHEESE

1 EGG WHITE

1 CUP CHOPPED DRIED APRICOTS

1 CUP ALL-PURPOSE FLOUR

⅛ TEASPOON SALT

PREHEAT THE OVEN to 375°F. Put the almonds in the bowl of a food processor fitted with a blade attachment and process for 1 minute to achieve a fine meal. Remove the almond meal and set aside. Put the butter, goat cheese, and ⅓ cup of the almond meal back into the bowl, and process until smooth. Add the egg white and the apricots. Process for 20 seconds. Be careful not to overprocess or the apricots will not be distinct small pieces in the dough. Add the flour and salt and process just until the mixture forms into a dough.

SPRINKLE A CLEAN WORK SURFACE with some of the remaining almond meal. Put the dough on top and press it into a small rectangle. Dust the top of the dough liberally with almond meal and roll it into a 6-by-12-inch bar about ½ inch thick. Add more almond meal on top of the dough and underneath it to prevent it from sticking to the work surface or rolling pin, if needed. Trim the dough to an exact rectangle and cut into ½-inch bars using a pizza cutter.

CAREFULLY LIFT AND PLACE the cookie bars on an ungreased baking sheet and bake until the cookies look barely browned, 10 to 12 minutes. Remove the baking sheet from the oven and place on a cooling rack. Serve at room temperature and store any leftovers airtight at room temperature for up to 3 days.

WALNUT RUGALACH

This flaky rolled dough makes a traditional Hanukkah bite-sized, crescent-shaped cookie. Classic cream-cheese pastry tastes great with the fresh walnut pesto filling. Make plenty and serve with salad.

FILLING

1 CUP PACKED FRESH BASIL LEAVES, RINSED AND DRIED

1 GARLIC CLOVE, PEELED AND FINELY CHOPPED

½ CUP EXTRA-VIRGIN OLIVE OIL

¼ CUP WALNUT PIECES

⅛ TEASPOON SALT

¼ CUP FINELY GRATED PARMESAN CHEESE
(see page 24)

COOKIE DOUGH

½ CUP (1 STICK) UNSALTED BUTTER AT ROOM TEMPERATURE

4 OUNCES CREAM CHEESE AT ROOM TEMPERATURE

1 CUP UNBLEACHED ALL-PURPOSE FLOUR

TO PREPARE THE FILLING, put the basil, garlic, olive oil, walnuts, salt, and cheese in the bowl of a food processor fitted with a blade attachment and pulse to a uniform texture. Place the walnut pesto in a covered container and refrigerate until you're ready to assemble the cookies (see *Note*).

TO PREPARE THE COOKIE DOUGH, put the butter and cream cheese in the bowl of a food processor fitted with a blade attachment and blend together, about 1 minute. Scrape the sides of the bowl with a rubber spatula. Add the flour and blend until the mixture just starts forming into a dough. Wrap in plastic film and flatten to about a 1-inch-thick disc. Refrigerate until firm, about half an hour.

REMOVE THE DOUGH from the refrigerator, unwrap, and cut in half. Place half of the dough on a floured work surface. Lightly flour the top and press down gently to flatten it slightly. Roll into an 8-inch circle, about ¼ inch thick. Spread half of the pesto over the surface of the dough. Using a paring knife or pizza wheel, cut the circle into twelve equal wedges. Starting at the wide end, roll up each wedge and curve the ends to form crescents. Repeat with the other half of the dough.

PREHEAT THE OVEN to 350°F and line the bottom of a baking sheet with parchment paper or a nonstick baking mat. Place the cookies 1 inch apart on the prepared baking sheet. Center the baking sheet in the oven and bake until lightly browned, about 15 minutes. Transfer the cookies to a rack to cool. Serve warm or at room temperature. Store airtight at room temperature for up to 4 days.

NOTE

A good-quality, store-purchased pesto helps to cut the preparation time. Try sun-dried tomato or olive pesto as an alternative.

Classically made pesto will have a superb flavor. To make it, put all the ingredients in a mortar and grind with a pestle. Make your pesto in the food processor if you do not have a mortar and pestle. Cilantro, mint, sage, parsley, or arugula are great alternatives for the basil.

SAUCES

SPREADS

CHUTNEYS

SALADS

THE SIDE SHOW

These tasty accompaniments have one thing in common—their versatility. They can go on the side of or inside many of the recipes in this book, or they can be used with your own favorite dish. Try filling the Chili-Grilled Eggplant Tartlets (page 60) with a dollop of Ricotta Filling, or smear Fig and Rosemary Spread inside Sour Cream Fig Spirals (page 132) just before rolling them up, or accompany Buckwheat Blinis with Warm Bing Cherries (page 43). Enjoy them however you like!

APPLE, PEAR, AND GINGER CHUTNEY

MAKES

2

CUPS

I like this slightly milder version of chutney, which can accompany a variety of savory biscuits, muffins, scones, crackers, or cookies. Try my version in the center of the Pecan Thumbprints (page 127), spooned on Five-Spice Black-and-White Sesame Wafers (page 135), or spread inside Orange-Nutmeg Popovers (page 105).

½ CUP FINELY DICED RED BELL PEPPER

1 RED DELICIOUS APPLE, PEELED, CORED, AND DICED

2 GRANNY SMITH APPLES, PEELED, CORED, AND DICED

2 PEARS, PEELED, CORED, AND DICED

½ CUP DRIED CURRANTS OR RAISINS

¼ CUP MINCED PEELED FRESH GINGER

1 TABLESPOON GRATED LEMON ZEST

1 TABLESPOON GRATED ORANGE ZEST

2 TABLESPOONS APPLE CIDER VINEGAR

¾ CUP WATER

⅓ CUP LIGHT BROWN SUGAR

½ TEASPOON GROUND CINNAMON

¼ TEASPOON GROUND CORIANDER

¼ TEASPOON GROUND CUMIN

¼ TEASPOON CURRY POWDER

¼ TEASPOON DRIED MUSTARD

⅛ TEASPOON GROUND ALLSPICE

STIR ALL THE INGREDIENTS together in a large, heavy-gauge, wide-bottomed saucepan. Cover with a lid and bring the mixture to a boil over high heat; reduce the heat to medium and cook for 1 hour. During the cooking process, stir occasionally and check to see that the liquid has not evaporated completely. Add a little water if the mixture looks completely dry. Remove the chutney from the pan and let cool at room temperature. Serve at room temperature or chilled.

NOTE

Store wrapped airtight in the refrigerator for up to 2 weeks. The chutney will become more flavorful as it sits.

FIG AND ROSEMARY SPREAD

MAKES

2½

CUPS

This aromatic fig-sweetened spread can be spooned on or inside cookies, eaten with crackers, or served with cheese.

1 POUND DRIED MISSION FIGS (ABOUT 2½ CUPS)

2 TABLESPOONS FINELY CHOPPED FRESH ROSEMARY

½ TEASPOON SALT

½ TEASPOON FRESHLY GROUND BLACK PEPPER

ZEST OF 1 LARGE ORANGE

1 CUP FRESH ORANGE JUICE

1 TABLESPOON CLOVER HONEY

½ CUP WATER

PUT THE FIGS, rosemary, salt, pepper, orange zest, orange juice, honey, and water in a medium saucepan over medium heat. Cover the pan and bring to a boil; reduce the heat to low and simmer the figs until the liquid is thick, about 30 minutes. Watch carefully while cooking so all the liquid does not evaporate.

REMOVE THE PAN from the heat and drain the figs, reserving the liquid. If needed, add additional water to the fig liquid to total ¾ cup. Put the figs and liquid in the bowl of a food processor fitted with a blade attachment and process until smooth, about 1 minute, scraping the sides of the bowl once or twice. Store the fig spread in an airtight container, refrigerated, for up to 1 week, or freeze for up to 2 months.

TAPENADE CREAM

Use this versatile cream as a spread, dip, or filling. Try spreading it inside the Walnut Rugalach (page 139) or serve it alongside a savory cookie assortment for dipping.

ONE 8-OUNCE PACKAGE CREAM CHEESE AT ROOM TEMPERATURE

1 TABLESPOON EXTRA-VIRGIN OLIVE OIL

¼ TEASPOON FRESHLY GROUND WHITE PEPPER

¼ TEASPOON GARLIC POWDER

½ TEASPOON DRIED OREGANO

1 TEASPOON FRESH LEMON JUICE

1 TABLESPOON CAPERS, DRAINED AND RINSED

½ CUP GREEN OLIVES, RINSED

½ CUP KALAMATA OLIVES, RINSED

¼ CUP CHOPPED RED BELL PEPPERS

PUT THE CREAM CHEESE, olive oil, pepper, garlic powder, oregano, lemon juice, and capers in the bowl of a food proccssor. Process until smooth, scraping the sides of the bowl occasionally. Add the olives and process for about 30 seconds. Add the red peppers and process for another 10 seconds. Store the tapenade cream in an airtight container for up to 1 week, refrigerated, or freeze for up to 1 month.

TROPICAL FRUIT RELISH

Finely dice the fruits or cut them into chunks, whichever you prefer. Serve with grilled fish, tortilla chips, or Coconut Shrimp Fritters (page 107).

1 CUP PEELED AND FINELY CHOPPED FRESH PINEAPPLE

1 RIPE MANGO, PEELED AND FINELY CHOPPED

¼ CUP FINELY CHOPPED RED BELL PEPPER

4 SCALLIONS, WHITE AND GREEN PARTS, CHOPPED

2 TABLESPOONS MINCED AND PEELED FRESH GINGER

1 TABLESPOON FINELY CHOPPED JALAPEÑO PEPPER

¼ CUP LIGHT COCONUT MILK

1 TABLESPOON TIGHTLY PACKED LIGHT BROWN SUGAR

JUICE AND ZEST OF ONE LIME

SALT

STIR ALL THE INGREDIENTS together in a medium bowl. Serve immediately or cover and refrigerate for up to 3 days.

RICOTTA FILLING AND DIP

This filling and dip can be used in many of your favorite recipes, including lasagna, stuffed shells, or even stuffed chicken breast. For a creamier version, use whole-milk ricotta cheese and heavy (whipping) cream. Add additional lemon and garlic for a zestier-flavored cool dip. Serve on crackers, with crudités, or inside the Chili-Grilled Eggplant and Sweet Roasted Pepper Tartlets in Poppy Seed Shells (page 60).

1 CUP PART-SKIM RICOTTA CHEESE

2 TEASPOONS FINELY GRATED LEMON ZEST

1 TEASPOON FRESH LEMON JUICE

2 TABLESPOONS FINELY CHOPPED FRESH PARSLEY

2 TABLESPOONS FINELY CHOPPED RED BELL PEPPER

¼ TEASPOON GARLIC POWDER

1 TABLESPOON WHOLE MILK

SALT

1 TABLESPOON TOASTED SESAME SEEDS FOR GARNISH (*optional*)

PUT ALL THE INGREDIENTS, except the sesame seeds, in a small bowl and stir well to combine. Spoon into a serving dish and sprinkle with toasted sesame seeds, if desired.

NOTE

Prepare the filling up to 4 days ahead. Cover and refrigerate until needed. Stir well and serve chilled or at room temperature.

WARM BING CHERRIES

Use fresh cherries when they are available or canned sweet dark cherries (see Note). Serve with blinis and a dollop of Crème Fraîche (facing page) or with pork roast or duck.

1½ CUPS FRESH BING CHERRIES, PITTED

1 TABLESPOON WATER

¼ CUP DRY RED WINE

2 TABLESPOONS BALSAMIC VINEGAR

1 TEASPOON FINELY CHOPPED FRESH THYME

2 TEASPOONS CORNSTARCH

½ TEASPOON GRATED LEMON ZEST

1 TABLESPOON CLOVER HONEY

PUT ALL THE INGREDIENTS in a small saucepan over medium heat. Stir and bring the mixture to a boil. Reduce the heat to low and simmer for 10 minutes; the liquid will look shiny and thick. Serve warm or cold. Store in the refrigerator covered for up to 1 week.

NOTE

When fresh cherries are not in season, substitute one 15.25-ounce can dark sweet cherries, drained. Omit the water and increase the cornstarch to 1 tablespoon.

CRÈME FRAÎCHE

Make your own crème fraîche for a superb garnish.

2 CUPS HEAVY (WHIPPING) CREAM
4 TABLESPOONS BUTTERMILK

STIR THE CREAM AND BUTTERMILK together in a small saucepan. Warm over low heat but do not bring to a boil. Pour the warm liquid into a small container and cover. Store at room temperature until thick, 8 to 48 hours. Once the crème fraîche is thick, cover and keep refrigerated for up to 1 week.

APRICOT-MINT RELISH

This fresh, cool relish nicely complements Mustard-Rubbed Mini Lamb Sandwiches on Mint Shortcakes (page 87) or a roasted leg of lamb.

1 CUP DICED AND PITTED FRESH APRICOTS

¼ CUP CHOPPED DRIED APRICOTS

¼ CUP FINELY CHOPPED RED ONION

¼ CUP ROASTED RED PEPPER FROM A JAR (DRAINED AND DICED)

¼ CUP DICED FRESH RED BELL PEPPER

2 TABLESPOONS SHERRY WINE VINEGAR

2 TABLESPOONS EXTRA-VIRGIN OLIVE OIL

¼ TEASPOON CURRY POWDER

¼ TEASPOON DRIED MUSTARD

½ TEASPOON GRANULATED SUGAR

3 TABLESPOONS CHOPPED FRESH MINT

SALT

MIX ALL THE INGREDIENTS except the salt in a medium bowl. Add salt to taste. Cover and store in the refrigerator for up to 2 days.

SMOKY TOMATO SAUCE

Smoked paprika and the fire-roasted tomatoes blend delightfully well, creating a light, sweet sauce versatile enough to accompany Shiitake Mushroom and Garlic Soufflés (page 117) or Grilled-Vegetable Galette (page 81), or simply to be ladled over fresh pasta.

3 TABLESPOONS UNSALTED BUTTER

1 SMALL ONION, FINELY DICED

SALT AND FRESHLY GROUND BLACK PEPPER

2 GARLIC CLOVES, MINCED

¾ TEASPOON SMOKED PAPRIKA

¼ CUP DRY WHITE WINE

ONE 32-OUNCE CAN DICED FIRE-ROASTED TOMATOES

½ CUP CHICKEN BROTH

1 BAY LEAF

4 SPRIGS FRESH THYME

MELT THE BUTTER in a medium saucepan over medium heat. Add the onions and a pinch of salt and pepper. Sauté until the onions are soft and translucent, about 5 minutes. Add the garlic and paprika and sauté for 30 seconds. Add the wine and reduce by half. Add the tomatoes, broth, and herbs. Reduce the heat and simmer until the sauce thickens, about 30 minutes. Pick out and discard the herbs and pour the tomato sauce into a blender. Purée the sauce until it is smooth. Season to taste with additional salt and pepper, if needed.

THE SAUCE CAN BE COVERED and refrigerated for up to 1 week. Make a big batch of sauce and freeze for up to 1 month.

CHILI-GRILLED EGGPLANT AND SWEET ROASTED PEPPERS

I keep this healthful dip (or filling) as a staple in my household. Chili oil, cumin, and garlic are natural complements to grilled eggplant and sweet roasted peppers. If you'd like an extra kick, add a little more chili oil. Serve as a dip or as a filling for the Chili-Grilled Eggplant and Sweet Roasted Peppers Tartlets in Poppy Seed Shells (page 60).

1 POUND EGGPLANT (ABOUT 2 MEDIUM)

¼ CUP CHILI OIL

¼ CUP PLUS 2 TABLESPOONS EXTRA-VIRGIN OLIVE OIL

¼ TO ½ TEASPOON GROUND CUMIN

SALT

1 MEDIUM RED BELL PEPPER (*see* Note)

1 MEDIUM YELLOW BELL PEPPER (*see* Note)

1 SMALL CLOVE GARLIC, MINCED

2 TABLESPOONS BALSAMIC VINEGAR

PREHEAT THE GRILL to medium. Slice the eggplant into ¼-inch-thick slices and put the slices on a baking sheet. Stir the chili oil and the ¼ cup olive oil together in a small bowl. Lightly brush both sides of the eggplant slices with the oil mixture and dust with a little ground cumin and salt.

HEAT THE GRILL. Place the eggplant and peppers on the grill. Roast the eggplant until soft and well marked by the grill, about 2 minutes on each side. Remove from the grill to cool. Roast the peppers until black on all sides, 10 to 12 minutes. Remove from the grill and let cool. Peel the black skin off the peppers and then stem, derib, and take out the seeds. Put the eggplant slices, the remaining

2 tablespoons olive oil, half of each of the roasted peppers, garlic, and a little salt in the bowl of a food processor. Pulse until chunky, 5 to 10 seconds. Remove from the bowl and season with more salt, if desired.

CUT THE REMAINING roasted peppers into julienne strips and toss with the balsamic vinegar. Garnish the eggplant mixture with the julienned balsamic peppers. Store in the refrigerator covered for up to 1 week.

NOTE

Purchased jarred or canned roasted red and yellow peppers can be used to save time.

ARUGULA SALAD WITH FETA-CORN VINAIGRETTE

Serve this fresh salad with lots of the dishes in this book or with your favorite barbecued entrée. I really like it with Seafood Strudel (page 69).

2 EARS FRESH CORN, HUSKS AND SILK REMOVED

¼ CUP EXTRA-VIRGIN OLIVE OIL, PLUS MORE FOR BRUSHING

3 TABLESPOONS SHERRY WINE VINEGAR

1 TABLESPOON CHOPPED FRESH TARRAGON

⅓ CUP CRUMBLED FETA CHEESE

SALT AND FRESHLY GROUND BLACK PEPPER

6 OUNCES FRESH ARUGULA, RINSED AND DRIED

PREHEAT THE OVEN to 400°F. Brush the ears of corn with olive oil and wrap each ear in aluminum foil. Place into the oven for 20 minutes to roast. Remove from the oven and let cool.

WHISK THE OLIVE OIL, vinegar, and tarragon together. Toss in the feta cheese. Cut the corn from the cob and add it to the vinaigrette. Season to taste with salt and pepper. Divide the arugula among 4 plates and top with equal amounts of the corn vinaigrette.

CAPRESE SALAD

Use ripe summer tomatoes when they're available and fresh cow's milk mozzarella or buffalo mozzarella. Use as a filling for profiteroles (see page 108), spread on crostini, or serve by itself as a salad.

6 OUNCES FRESH MOZZARELLA, DICED INTO ¼-INCH CUBES

¾ CUP SEEDED AND CHOPPED FRESH TOMATOES

½ CUP PACKED CHOPPED FRESH BASIL LEAVES

2 TABLESPOONS EXTRA-VIRGIN OLIVE OIL

SALT AND FRESHLY GROUND BLACK PEPPER

TOSS ALL THE INGREDIENTS together in a medium bowl, seasoning to taste with the salt and pepper. Cover and store in the refrigerator for up to 2 days.

GLOSSARY

BEIGNET {ben-YAY}
Pieces of dough made of deep-fried pâte à choux paste, often containing sweet or savory fillings.

BETTY
Dating back to colonial America, betties are baked puddings made of layers of sugared and spiced fruit and buttered breadcrumbs. The most popular is apple brown betty.

BISCOTTI {bee-SKAWT-tee}
A crunchy, dry, twice-baked Italian cookie that is often dipped in coffee or sweet wine.

BISCUIT
A light-textured quick bread leavened with baking powder or baking soda. Biscuits are generally savory but can also be sweetened and served with fruit and whipped cream.

CAPRESE {kah-PRAY-say}
Related phrase "insalata caprese," literally, "the salad from Capri." A salad that is a perfect summer dish. Fresh tomatoes, buffalo or cow's milk mozzarella, and fresh basil are tossed together and finished with a drizzle of extra-virgin olive oil.

CHEESECAKE
A dense rich and creamy dessert usually made with cream cheese but sometimes ricotta cheese or cottage cheese. The batter is poured into a springform pan, baked, and cooled before cutting. Sour cream topping, whipped cream, or fruit are among the garnishes used for cheesecake.

CLAFOUTI {kla-foo-TEE}
Fresh cherries or plums are covered with an eggy, cakelike sweet batter in this dessert that originated in the Limousin region of France.

COBBLER
A deep-dish fruit dessert covered with a crust or cake. Originally, a cobbler's top crust consisted of thick spoonfuls of biscuit dough or dumplings that cooked on top of fruit. Eventually the dough evolved into a pie-crust type of covering that was rolled and fitted on top of the fruit and then baked.

CRÊPE {KRAYP; KREHP}
A light, thin French pancake served rolled or folded and containing sweet or savory fillings.

CRISP
A fruit dessert with a crunchy baked topping made of sugar, butter, and flour.

CRUMBLE
A British dessert of cut fruit topped with pastry containing oatmeal to help make it crumbly.

DUMPLING
Dessert dumplings are pastry dough wrapped around fruit and baked. Savory dumplings are mounds of dough, sometimes stuffed with meat or cheese, cooked in soup.

FRITTER
A small sweet or savory deep-fried dough mixed with chopped fruits or vegetables. A fritter can also mean any small deep-fried cake made from yeasted dough or choux paste.

GALETTE {gah-LET}
A flaky pastry or yeast dough served flat and topped with cheese, fruit, herbs, jam, meat, or nuts.

GRATIN {GRAH-ten}
A cheese- or buttered bread crumb–covered dish, broiled crispy.

HOLLANDAISE {HOL-uhn-dayz}
A creamy sauce made with butter, egg yolks, and lemon juice; it is served with savory dishes.

MADELEINE {MAD-l-ihn; mad-LEHN}
A petite cakelike cookie shaped like an elongated scallop shell.

MUFFIN
A cupcake-shaped quick bread, usually made slightly sweet and served for breakfast. Most muffins are leavened with baking powder or baking soda.

PANCAKE
A type of quick bread usually prepared from a batter that is cooked on a hot griddle or in a skillet. Pancakes have hundreds of variations and can be served for breakfast, lunch, and dinner, or as appetizers, entrées, and desserts.

PANCETTA {pan-CHEH-tuh}
Cured Italian bacon used for adding flavor to sauces, pasta dishes, and meat dishes.

PARMIGIANO-REGGIANO
{pahr-muh-ZHAH-noh reh-zhee-AH-noh}
An Italian hard, dry cheese made from skimmed or partially skimmed cow's milk. The two-to-four-year aging process produces a complex-flavored cheese with a grainy texture.

PHYLLO DOUGH

A water and flour dough rolled and stretched thin enough to see through. The dough is usually layered and used in many sweet and savory applications, such as strudel and baklava.

POPOVER

Thin popover batters bake into puffy, crisp-shelled, and semihollow quick breads; usually served as a side dish.

POTPIE

A type of sweet or savory pie often baked in pie plates and in single-serving size.

PROFITEROLE {*Fr. Proh-FIH-ter-ohl; It. Pro-fee-the-ROH-leh*}

A tiny cream puff made from pâte à choux paste, filled with sweet or savory fillings and served for dessert or hors d'oeuvres.

PROSCIUTTO {*proh-SHOO-toh*}

Salt-cured, air-dried Italian ham.

PUTTANESCA {*poot-tah-NEHS-kah*} SAUCE

A spicy sauce of anchovies, black olives, capers, garlic, onions, oregano, and tomatoes cooked together in olive oil.

QUICHE {*KEESH*}

A versatile savory pie usually made in a pie shell lined with pie dough. Fillings consist of eggs, milk or cream, and a variety of cheeses, meats, vegetables, or herbs.

RELISH

A condiment usually made with chopped vegetables or fruit and served uncooked, lightly cooked, or pickled. It can be smooth or chunky, sweet or savory, hot or mild.

RUGALACH {*RUHG-uh-luhkh*}

Small and crescent-shaped, these cookies contain fillings of jam, nuts, poppy seeds, or raisins. A traditional Hanukkah cookie.

SCONE {*SKOHN*}

A quick bread usually cut into triangles or rounds before baking. Scones are popular for breakfast or tea and are usually slightly sweetened. Savory scones can contain a variety of herbs, cheeses, spices, or vegetables.

SHORTBREAD COOKIE

A rich cookie made with butter, flour, and sugar. Shortbread cookies are formed into squares, triangles, or rounds and baked to a light brown color.

SHORTCAKE

A tender biscuitlike or sponge cake–textured quick bread topped with sweet or savory fillings. Strawberry shortcake is made with a shortcake base crowned with fresh whipped cream and strawberry slices.

SOUFFLÉ {*soo-FLAY*}

A soufflé is made by folding whipped egg whites into a thick sauce-type base and then baking in the oven. It rises to two times its original size, creating a light, airy sweet or savory meal or dessert.

STRUDEL {*STROOD-l; SHTROO-duhl*}

Wafer-thin layers of pastry dough spread with sweet or savory fillings, rolled into logs, and baked to a golden brown.

TART/TARTLET

Open-faced, straight-sided pies made with a sweet dough or savory dough crust. Tarts are usually filled with custards, fruits, or savory fillings. They are made in a variety of sizes from petite to 14 inches in diameter.

TUILE {*TWEEL*}

A thin, crisp French cookie classically made with crushed almonds. Tuiles are baked and many times placed over a dowel rod to form a curved shape.

TURNOVER

Crisp-shelled pastry triangles with sweet or savory fillings and are baked or fried. Served as appetizers, entrées, or desserts.

WAFFLE

A light quick bread batter-type cake cooked in a waffle iron, which gives a distinct honeycomb pattern to the cake. Waffles are popular for breakfast but can be served as an entrée or for dessert.

INDEX

C

TABLE OF EQUIVALENTS

The exact equivalents in the following tables have been rounded for convenience.

LIQUID/DRY MEASUREMENTS

U.S.	METRIC
¼ teaspoon	1.25 milliliters
½ teaspoon	2.5 milliliters
1 teaspoon	5 milliliters
1 tablespoon (3 teaspoons)	15 milliliters
1 fluid ounce (2 tablespoons)	30 milliliters
¼ cup	60 milliliters
⅓ cup	80 milliliters
½ cup	120 milliliters
1 cup	240 milliliters
1 pint (2 cups)	480 milliliters
1 quart (4 cups, 32 ounces)	960 milliliters
1 gallon (4 quarts)	3.84 liters
1 ounce (by weight)	28 grams
1 pound	448 grams
2.2 pounds	1 kilogram

LENGTHS

U.S.	METRIC
⅛ inch	3 millimeters
¼ inch	6 millimeters
½ inch	12 millimeters
1 inch	2.5 centimeters

OVEN TEMPERATURE

FAHRENHEIT	CELSIUS	GAS
250	120	½
275	140	1
300	150	2
325	160	3
350	180	4
375	190	5
400	200	6
425	220	7
450	230	8
475	240	9
500	260	10

31901046547495